seconds to snap

One Explosive Day. A Family Destroyed.
My Descent into Anorexia

Tina McGuff with Katy Weitz

JOHN BLAKE

Published by John Blake Publishing Ltd,
3 Bramber Court, 2 Bramber Road,
London W14 9PB, England

www.johnblakebooks.com

www.facebook.com/johnblakebooks **f**
twitter.com/jblakebooks **t**

This edition published in 2015

ISBN: 978 1 78418 382 0

British Library Cataloguing-in-Publication Data:

A catalogue record for this book is available from the British Library.

Design by www.envydesign.co.uk

Printed in Great Britain by CPI Group (UK) Ltd

1 3 5 7 9 10 8 6 4 2

The right of Tina McGuff and Katy Weitz to be identified as the authors
of this work has been asserted by them in accordance with the

Papers ... ... ducts
made fron ... ... rocesses
confo ... ... gin.

Every at ... ... olders,

What lies behind us and what lies before us are tiny matters
compared to what lies within us.
Richard Waldo Emerson

You have brains in your head.
You have feet in your shoes.
You can steer yourself
any direction you choose.
You're on your own.
And you know what you know.
And YOU are the one who'll decide where to go…
Oh! The Places You'll Go!, Dr. Seuss

Seconds to Snap is dedicated to all those who live under
the cloud of shame and fear.
Have faith, trust and hang in there. It's time to tell your story.

Contents

Prologue

The early morning sun catches the crests of the waves of the North Sea, sending out tiny sparks that dance across the water as our car speeds past the coastline. Beside me in the driver's seat is my husband Jock and behind us three of our four children – Danny, twenty-three, John, seventeen, and Holli, fifteen. We are on our way to Aberdeen for a reunion with a dear family friend – Brodie. My eyes drift to the road and I see the sign for Fordoun. *Fordoun*! I haven't thought of this place in years! Instantly, I am transported back 20 years when I piloted a plane to the small runway here. My skin shivers with excitement once more as I recall the moment I caught sight of the landing strip, the feeling of elation at successfully flying on my own, the wonder of seeing this incredible planet from a bird's eye perspective. I swell inside. I remember the feeling I had then and the voice that spoke to me in my head: *Look what I have done! Look what I can do when I put my mind to it!*

In the car, I turn around to look at my children: John with his iPod on, slowly rocking to an unknown rhythm, Danny staring out the window, drinking in the rugged and beautiful surroundings, and Holli engrossed in her book. *Look what I have done*, I say to myself now and once more I am touched with a mixture of pride and awe. They catch me looking at them and John's eyes meet mine. He releases a gentle smile so sweet and loving it pierces my heart.

I feel a tiny prickle behind my eyes. It's a fleeting, intense but exquisite moment of happiness and I reach out to touch my husband's hand. He keeps his eyes on the road but he squeezes my fingers, returning my loving gesture. *You're okay, Tina*, I hear the voice inside my head speak to me. *You are okay and everything is going to be okay.*

If you had asked me years before if I ever saw a future like this, I would have laughed. Mirthlessly. It is deeply sad to admit but I didn't believe I was capable of becoming a happy or successful adult, parent or wife. In my darkest moments I thought death was the *only* option. Never in a million years could I have imagined this journey with my family, this feeling sweeping through me now of pure, unadulterated joy. And so it is these moments I cherish the most, the small daily reminders that I have come so far and achieved more than I ever dreamed possible. I know in my heart that life is a precious gift and I am grateful every day to be here, to have these feelings and to experience all that life has to offer.

Throughout my mental illness as a child, teenager and young

woman, I was in the care of professional, dedicated people who saved my life over and over again. They gave me the strength to hang on against the odds. It was not an easy road to travel, but one that had to be made. And to that end I would like to thank them from the bottom of my heart. They showed me there were so many magical and incredible moments that go towards making life a wondrous journey. And now I can experience them for myself, I feel truly blessed.

Today, I want to offer hope to others struggling with these terrible and often terrifying conditions. Don't lose hope! Never give up! There is always something to live for and even though it is not always possible to see your future through the darkness and the fear, hang onto the thought one day it will change. IT WILL CHANGE. IT WILL GET BETTER. I never thought it would take me seconds to snap and years to recover but I made it and here is my story.

Tina McGuff, June 2015

Chapter 1

The Unkindest Cut

I was woken by a tap on my shoulder. Blinking open my eyes, I saw it was Dave, our family friend and neighbour. *Dave?* The light from the landing streamed in behind his tall frame. *What is Dave doing in my room? Where is my mum? Am I dreaming?*

Very calmly he leaned into me and said in a soft voice: 'There has been an accident. Get your sisters and come with me.'

I nodded, to show I understood but, all of a sudden, I felt scared – Dave already had my three-year-old sister Celine in his arms, fast asleep, and he stood waiting as I roused my two other sisters, who were in the double bed next to mine. Each looked confused and bleary-eyed as I gave them a little shake and then, once we were all up, standing in the middle of the room, barefoot in our Tinker Bell nighties, Dave led us across the landing to the stone spiral staircase with white steel balustrades.

'What's happening?' whispered my ten-year-old sister, Katie, clinging to my left arm as if she wanted to pull it off. Sophie, just seven, held onto my right arm with equal force, still too numb with sleep to speak.

'I don't know, but don't worry,' I tried to reassure her in my calm, adult voice. 'Everything's going to be okay, I promise.'

As we walked slowly down the cold stone stairs I saw four policemen staring at us all with pity and sadness in their eyes and two people in ordinary clothes. *What is happening? Why are they here and where is Mum and Dad?*

Suddenly, I noticed the red bloody handprints on the white-painted doorway and my heart began to race. Once at the bottom of the stairs, I went to walk through to the hall to get my school uniform but a police officer stood in my way.

Dave called out behind me: 'Forget the clothes, we'll come back for those.'

Now I saw more blood marks on the doorframe – they were everywhere. *What happened here? Where are Mum and Dad?* At that moment, everything felt so strange and wrong I couldn't help myself. I burst into tears and ran out of the house.

Outside, the cool summer night enveloped me. Cold and damp with the heavy scent of darkness, it wrapped me up like a blanket and for a moment I stopped crying. I just stood there on the pavement, my chest heaving. Each sister ran up behind me then grabbed my hand again. I couldn't let them see me like this – I couldn't let them down; I knew Dave was depending on me to keep them calm. But as we crossed the road to Dave's parents-in-law's flat opposite our own flat, I could feel myself shaking inside.

Dave and Suzie were our parents' good friends, and Suzie's parents, Maria and Alfonso, lived right across the road from us in a lovely flat. But I didn't see them – it was Suzie who met us at the front door and exchanged a quick, worried glance with Dave. They led us quietly up the stairs and into the spare room, showing us to the large double bed, where the others climbed in and immediately snuggled down under the large fluffy duvet.

'Don't worry,' she whispered to me as I looked at them questioningly. 'We'll take Celine back to ours tonight. Your parents are okay and you'll see them soon. We'll explain everything in the morning. Just try and get some sleep now.'

Then they crept out of the room and shut the door carefully behind them. Climbing into the big bed beside my sisters, I wrapped a protective arm around each one. I held them tightly, trying not to imagine the horrors that might have happened in my house and prayed my parents were indeed okay.

The room was light with the moon shining through the thin curtains. Maria had recently had it fitted with cream furniture and the place smelled like new wood. The walls were dotted with family pictures and religious paintings of Jesus and the Virgin Mary. I looked at the pictures and silently prayed to God, asking Him to make sure that my mum and dad were okay. I felt safe in this flat – Maria and Alfonso were kind, loving people who ran a fish-and-chip shop, where I often helped out at weekends. When we finished our late shift, I would often stay here overnight so as not to disturb my parents, so this place was familiar to me. Their flat, and especially this room, felt warm and comforting. But my mind was a whir. For a long while, I just lay awake, staring at the pictures on the walls, listening to the sounds of my sisters' soft breathing beside me.

I must have fallen asleep eventually because I was woken by Suzie in the morning, with a gentle hand on my shoulder.

'Morning, Tina – are you okay?' she asked, smiling, her dark eyes crinkling in the corners, framed by her shoulder-length auburn hair. Suzie's family was Italian and she always looked very beautiful and exotic to me.

I nodded briefly – in a flash, the strange events from last night tumbled back into my mind, my limbs felt heavy and I was overcome by a horrible sense that things were definitely not okay.

'Would you like some breakfast?'

I followed Suzie through to the lounge, where I saw my sisters were already up and munching their way through large bowls of cornflakes. Just seeing them at the table like this, eating normally, immediately made me feel a little better but still there was a knot of anxiety in the pit of my stomach. Suzie brought me a bowl of cornflakes and I sat with the others, eating slowly. I had no appetite.

Once the others had left the table and were seated round the TV watching Maria's favourite video, *Calamity Jane*, I beckoned Suzie over. She was wearing a smart, crisp white shirt tucked into blue jeans and her earrings jangled prettily when she moved.

'Can you tell me what happened, please?' I asked.

Suzie quickly put her head down: 'Dave will be back shortly and he will explain everything.'

Suddenly, the knot in my stomach clenched painfully. *Why*

won't she talk to me about it? What's happened? I looked down at my half-finished bowl of cornflakes but I knew I couldn't eat another mouthful. Fear gripped me tightly and wouldn't let go. All I wanted was to go home and for everything to be back to normal. I wanted my mum and dad back again so that we could just carry on being a happy, loving family. I couldn't understand what might have happened – my mum and dad were madly in love and loved us, too. We thought they were the most beautiful, wonderful parents in the world. My dad was always happy, singing all the time, and my mum was an elegant, loving, adoring mother, whom we idolised. But where were they now?

An hour later, there was a knock at the front door and Suzie left to open it. From the living room, I heard a lot of hushed talk in the hallway, whispered urgent voices. Now I wanted to cry – I was desperate to know something, anything at all, but it was all being kept from us. Katie and Sophie clamoured for me to do their hair – all of us had long, white hair, which Mum normally plaited or braided into pigtails. But today there was no Mum and the realisation made me all the more miserable. Reluctantly, I brushed, pulled and weaved my sisters' hair into their requested styles but my stomach continued to churn with anxiety.

Eventually, I heard the front door close and Suzie returned to the living room. Quietly, I sidled up to her.

'How long will Dave be?' I asked. I was scared but I didn't want to let my sisters hear the fear in my voice. At thirteen, I was the eldest and I knew they were looking to me to show them there was nothing to be frightened of. They were my main concern now and I had to ensure they were safe and sound.

'He won't be long – he's on his way,' she replied quickly, then left the room again, saying she needed to go to the bathroom. Her voice sounded strange and I could tell she was reluctant to look me in the eye, which made me feel increasingly uneasy. Why would Suzie be so uncomfortable around me? I felt sick; I had never felt so scared before in all my life and not knowing what was going on was burning a hole in my tummy. I could feel the tears swell behind my eyes but I fought them back with all my might, taking in long, deep breaths. This was the worst feeling in the world.

At some point, Maria and Alfonso appeared and started bustling around, then Suzie brought our clothes over from across the street and we all changed into our jeans and T-shirts. At around midday, Dave arrived. He was wearing a red-checked shirt and his light blue eyes were clouded with worry. I waited patiently as he greeted the adults, watching him out of the corner of my eye while pretending to watch TV.

Eventually, he came over to me and quietly, so the others couldn't hear, he said: 'Tina, can I have a word with you next door?'

I followed him silently into the hallway and through to the room that Maria called her 'antiques room'. She was a collector and the room was stuffed to the brim with the most wonderful old clocks, furniture, vases and chairs. It was an Aladdin's cave, a treasure trove but, right now, I hardly took notice of the old wooden furniture around me and just plonked myself down on the cold cream-leather sofa.

Dave came and sat down beside me.

'Tina,' he started slowly. 'Last night, your mum hurt your dad . . .'

He didn't get any further – the tears I'd been fighting back all morning suddenly welled up and spilled out of me in a giant sob. I crumpled up and buried my head in my hands. Dave put a comforting arm around me.

'Shhhh now,' he said softly. 'Don't worry. Everything is going to be okay. Just try to stay calm.'

But I knew at that moment nothing would ever be the same again. My head span, I felt sick and terrified at the same time. Our lives had changed and the happy family I had once known was now gone for ever. I sat like that for some time, weeping into my hands, until eventually, Dave said he had to get back to the others.

'Just try and be strong,' he said. 'You'll see your mum and dad again soon, I promise.'

And that was it: he left. I ran into the bathroom and locked the door. I had to pull myself together for the sake of my sisters. They couldn't see me in this state or they would panic, too. So I ran the cold tap and dipped my hands in, splashing water over my face once, twice, three times, until the heat in my cheeks cleared a little and I started to calm down.

I looked up at the small mirror, into my puffy, bloodshot eyes and pink, tear-stained cheeks, and willed myself to calm down. It couldn't have been more than ten minutes that I was in there, but it felt like for ever.

You can't let them see you like this, I told myself sternly. *Don't let them know you are sad. Just be brave. Be brave!*

Even as I said those words to myself, I felt the tears bubbling up inside me again but I pushed them back and patted my wet face with the soft cream hand cloth.

I thought back to the day before. Everything had seemed so normal. I'd got in from school as usual and Mum was making tea in the kitchen while Dad was in the living room, listening to his Neil Diamond records. They had both been working hard recently – Mum with her beauty salon and Dad with his painting-and-decorating business. But it all seemed to be going so well. I couldn't understand how it had come to this. Mum looked like a model, with long, strawberry-blonde hair and an amazing figure, always immaculately groomed. Dad was very handsome and a real gentleman. My sisters and I were always together playing and loved being with each other. Now, our lives were in tatters.

I gave a little involuntary shudder then I unlocked the door and went through to the living room, wearing a great big fake smile.

Chapter 2

Out of Africa

The days passed slowly without any sign of Mum and Dad and we fell into a routine of sorts, where I would go with Maria and Alfonso to the fish-and-chip shop to help out behind the counter, while my sisters stayed back at their flat. I didn't mind – I was so used to the place, it almost felt like a second home to me. As I sprinkled salt and vinegar on chips then folded them in newspaper, my mind wandered back over the last year, racking my brains to think of what could have prompted my mother to act so out of character.

We had only been back in Dundee just over a year after 5 years living in South Africa. We had moved to Pretoria on 5 August 1975, my sixth birthday, when my dad's new employer, Iscor, relocated us. It was a huge adventure. We had never been out of Dundee before, never even travelled on a plane before, and we were so excited by the promise of a new life abroad. We left a wet and grey Dundee and arrived at a very hot and sunny South Africa.

We moved straight in with my Uncle William, his wife, Cara, and their daughter, Sara, until we got a place of our own. Mum immediately landed a job as a Max Factor consultant for a department store in the heart of Pretoria, and loved it. Dad was also happy in his job with Iscor, a steel fabrication and production factory.

After a few months, we found our own place in Ingot Terrace, Westpark. It was a bungalow-style house, not far from Iscor, and life was good. Katie and I were sent to Burger Right Primary School. We had beautiful gingham uniforms with white ankle socks and black shoes. I loved the school – it had a massive sports stadium and there were cheerleaders, football teams, track and swimming. It was like something out of an American movie, nothing like Dundee! At the bottom of the school road there was a KFC, where we sometimes went as a treat on the way home.

Jacaranda and Mulberry trees surrounded the school and we used their leaves to feed the silk worms that all the kids collected and bred for fun. We had tons of caterpillars, which we swapped, in school, like kids in Dundee did with stickers and rubbers. They were really long and white, with touches of black. At home, we'd sit and watch for hours as they spun their beautiful silk cocoons. They were so soft and the thread was delicate and had a beautiful shimmer to it, like gold thread. Eventually, each worm would disappear into its cocoon and then slowly reappear as a huge beautiful moth that looked like beige velvet. Then they would lay eggs and start all over again. I had hundreds all the time and used to love watching the cycle.

We fitted in easily and enjoyed our new lives. The only strange thing about South Africa was the fact that most of the school children were Afrikaans and all white. I was horrified when I was told that whites and blacks were not allowed to mix. In fact, we were made to feel that the dark-skinned people were worthless and the whites were in charge and superior. It was all wrong and Mum and Dad hated it, too. For us it was very unfamiliar to see such a division wherever we went.

My sisters and I very quickly learned Afrikaans and spoke it fluently, sometimes going for days without speaking any English. As soon as we got home from school each afternoon, we would run into the house, change into our shorts and then run outside barefoot to play with our neighbours. It was a very free, happy life for a child. And since it was very hot all of the time, swimming was a massive part of our lives: everyone in our street, including us, had a pool.

The best pool was the one at the Iscor Club, a private members club with a huge hall, games rooms, pools and bars. We would go swimming and then go inside to get chips with soy sauce, hot dogs or grape-flavoured Fanta.

Once a fortnight, local black women came to the houses with their babies wrapped around their bodies in beautiful multi-coloured blankets, carrying massive boxes on their heads. When they brought them down they contained tons of hand-carved soapstone, ornaments and handmade wooden crafts. There were always lots to choose from. These women were very strong and their necks must have been made of steel to carry all their wares.

They would come in from the townships to sell to the houses. Mum bought a lot for the house from them. I thought these women were amazing – some of them carried two children at a time, one at the front and one at the back, and they walked for miles. Even the way they managed to bend down without dropping the boxes or their babies was so graceful.

We loved being in South Africa – we were carefree and the world around us was bright, hot and sunny all the time. We had two Labradors, called Snoopy and Doody, a Ridgeback called Chang and Mum's precious little Pomeranian, Trudy; also a couple of rabbits. We spent a lot of time with our animals in the garden, running around.

The fruit trees were wonderful – I didn't even know what a mango was before I went there. Now we ate figs, paw paws, guava, lychees and all sorts of other fresh fruit. We had sugar canes in the garden and we would cut them down and break them up, then suck and chew on the fibrous cane to get at the sweet sugar. It was like nectar. I loved eating the cane and we munched on them every day.

Elizabeth our maid cooked delicious meals for us. Oxtail and a porridge called mealie pap (maize) were my favourites. I used to love sitting with her in her little shack in the garden, eating with our hands; it was much better than eating at the table. We would have Koodo or Springbok meat with thick, dark gravy, easily absorbed into the fluffy mealie pap we'd scoop up into our hands.

Elizabeth had a little baby boy and she would hide him all the time for she was not allowed to have children while working. He was a tiny boy, with tiny black curls, and he was so cute. I liked sitting in her shed, watching him play on the metal-framed bed elevated by house bricks at each leg. She liked having it up high so it would 'keep her safe from the devil'. She always smelled of soap and was very clean all the time. Her small, bare-brick room had net curtains, religious pictures on the walls and some books but nothing else. There was no electricity in there and she had little candle lamps.

One day, I came home from school to find Mum storming about the place. She was furious because the lady across the road had reported her for allowing Elizabeth to eat at our table – she had spotted her through the window. The police came and gave Mum a stern warning that she would be fined a huge amount and Elizabeth would be taken, if it were to happen again. Mum never spoke to that lady again. Luckily, though, they never saw the baby or he would have been taken away. It was very distressing for all of us.

The meat in South Africa was very fresh and most of the people bought animals frozen whole or halved. In our own freezer, we would often have a whole half of a frozen pig. One particular day changed my life and my relationship with food for ever. I was at one of the neighbour's as usual one afternoon and suddenly my friend's dad reversed his truck into the back garden, with two huge pigs on the back. The pigs seemed very scared – going by the horrendous amount of noise and squealing and thrashing around they were making, they were obviously trying to get out. The dad and a few of his friends climbed onto the back of the truck, took out a handgun and shot one of the pigs right through the head. I was dumbstruck.

At that moment, the other pig jumped from the trailer and

ran away up the road. A few of the men started off after it in another vehicle, while the rest stayed and dragged the dead pig off the back of the truck. I was sure it was alive as I could see it moving as they hung it up from a tree. Then they sliced it open and all its innards fell out; it took them seconds. I stood rooted to the spot – unable to speak or move – I was so horrified by what I had seen. Eventually, the other pig was dragged back into the garden, squealing in terror. It kept thrashing around – in another second, they shot this one in the head with a handgun, too.

To everyone else, this seemed normal but I had never seen anything so evil and murderous. Until that moment, I had no connection between food and live animals; it was a huge shock. I ran home, crying my eyes out, and vowed never to eat meat again. For a long time, I couldn't get those pigs out of my head. Mum and Dad tried to reassure me that it was okay and that we were meant to eat animals and the pigs would not have suffered but I knew they had as I'd seen the fear in their eyes and heard their pitiful squeals.

Over the years, we had some wonderful family holidays, visiting Kruger National Park, where I saw wild animals that I had only seen in books before: elephants, rhinos, lions, snakes and all sorts of incredible creatures. We also travelled to Durban Beach a few times. The beach was beautiful but it was where I got most of my worst sunburn as the temperatures soared to 120 degrees on the hottest days. I was covered in unsightly massive freckles all over my face. I hated them so much! I had to get zinc all over my nose to try to protect it for it was continually being burned and blistered.

Our other outings were to the ice rink in Pretoria and to the Drive Inns to watch movies. As they started in the evenings, we'd go there in our pyjamas and Dad would put the backseat of the car down flat with our covers and pillows so we could fall asleep during the film. I'll never forget watching *Grease* there and actually seeing Sandy at the Drive Inn at the same time we were in one, too! Eventually, we'd all drop off and Mum and Dad would carry us into our beds when we got home. When we woke in the morning, we'd have no memory of getting into bed!

We became obsessed by *Grease* the movie. Dad bought us the soundtrack and we listened to it over and over again until we knew all the words to the songs and then we pretended to be the characters and would dance and sing in the back garden. Dad always had Abba, Barry Manilow or Neil Diamond playing, or Mum played Rod Stewart on the record player.

One day, Mum announced she was pregnant and we were very excited, all of us secretly hoping for a brother. Celine, my new baby sister, was born on 17 January 1980 and, when I got home from school, Mum was sitting in the back garden holding her in a white shawl. We were all so excited to see her, we crowded around the tiny bundle, each of us desperate to peep at her scrunched-up little face and doll-like fists. I loved having a baby in the house – I was naturally very caring and nurturing since I was the eldest, and the baby brought us all closer together.

As for my parents – well, we were crazy about them. Especially Mum. When she came in from work, I'd run to her and give her a massive hug. She always smelled so good; she wore Cinnabar

15

perfume, which was musty and aromatic. The smell was like my comfort blanket. Mum had time for all of us and never held back with the kisses and affection – somehow, with four girls, she made each of us feel special and safe.

Celine was christened along with my other two sisters, Katie and Sophie, at our local church, where we always went for Sunday school. I wore my sequined Lucy Ewing outfit and a pair of glittery high-heel shoes to match. I must have looked ridiculous but Mum and Dad let me as I loved the TV soap *Dallas* so much and it made me happy.

By this time, Dad had changed jobs within the business and was training to be a painter and decorator. Mum was running her Max Factor section. But after five years, Dad's contract came to an end and he was offered tickets home for everyone, including a full relocation package. We were told very little of the move: we were so happy and contented, Mum did not want to upset us and, at first, going back to Dundee did seem like a real adventure.

We made the 20-hour journey home in 1981 and moved in with my gran, my dad's mum, while we found a place to live. Being back in Dundee was so far removed from what I remembered. Things looked different and much darker and, worst of all, we were freezing! Though at first it felt like a big holiday, after a few months the cold just seemed to seep into my bones and settle there.

We enrolled into a local primary school and, on the first day, everyone looked at us strangely as we must have stood out like sore thumbs. Mum had sent us into school with our Burger Right uniforms on, our hair was all long and white and we were covered in massive freckles. We spoke Afrikaans most of the time and took our shoes off at every opportunity. There were days we left school altogether to run home to Gran's house as we missed Pretoria. We didn't fit in at all and were baffled by our changed environment. Where were the outdoor pools, the trees, the insects and silk worms?

I struggled with all the subjects. School only starts in South Africa at six years old, so we were all about a year behind in our education and this increased my sense of loneliness and isolation. I knew nothing in the classes and felt so stupid but I made some lovely friends and they made me feel very welcome. However, I was trying to bluff my way through class as I had no idea what they were talking about. It made me panic about what was to come next – BIG SCHOOL!

Gradually, I became friends with a few boys and girls in the area and my whole world opened up to new experiences and new ways of thinking. After six months, we got our own place right next to Baxter Park – it was a beautiful Victorian house divided up into three flats. Our flat had two large bedrooms, both enormous, with high ceilings and original fireplaces. It was old but Mum had great taste and furnished it beautifully with elegant and expensive antiques. We had a huge red Chesterfield sofa in the lounge, a massive old wooden bureau and a green velvet chaise longue, scrumptious thick carpets, lovely rugs, flock wallpaper and beautiful Victorian fireguards.

The bedroom that I shared with my sisters was huge. Katie and Sophie slept in a double bed together, while I had my own single bed from Africa – a white metal frame with gold bed-end finials. Lying in it made me feel like a princess! We also had a huge walk-in wardrobe, where we kept all our clothes and toys, and a toilet outside our bedroom, a bit like an en suite. I even had my own phone. It was a green classic Trim line – sadly, it was not connected to a line. I had begged my parents to buy it for me because it was the same one Lucy Ewing had. I imagined myself as the Scottish Lucy Ewing – of course, without the oil, acres of land and sunshine!

Once I had finished primary school, I started at the local high school and, to begin with, I struggled to fit in. I was so far behind academically, I froze with fear whenever the teachers asked me a question. Mum had now at least bought me a new uniform and shoes, so I looked almost the same as everyone else, but I still spoke with a South African accent and was conscious that I looked out of place. I tried desperately to change the way I spoke, I was so desperate to make friends and fit in.

Eventually, my efforts paid off and I met a lovely friend called Susan, who took me to the Rollerama, a roller-skating rink in Dundee. It was brilliant! We hired four-wheeled skates and zoomed around to the music, like in a disco. I loved it, and Susan and I soon became very close friends. She went to a different school to me but lived just around the corner from us. We hung out nearly every night after school.

Mum opened up her beauty salon after eight months, which had sun beds, the new 'in thing', and offered makeovers, massage therapy and specialised skincare products. It was a lovely little shop. Meanwhile, my dad had started his painting-and-decorating business. They both seemed to be very happy and working hard. We saw them a bit less, as they tried to make their businesses work, and my granny – our dad's mum – looked after us, or our neighbours from across the road. After 18 months back in Dundee, it felt like we were finally settling down to our new lives.

Except something had suddenly gone terribly wrong – and I couldn't, for the life of me, work out what it could be.

After a few days with Maria and Alfonso, there was a knock at the door and my dad came in. He looked terrible – very pale and tired – but we were so happy to see him, we just flung ourselves into his arms and went mad, cuddling him. Eventually, he sat down on the couch but he did so very carefully, putting his hand back first to ease himself on. I could see from the tension in his body and the way he winced that he was in pain. Dave and Suzie came and sat down across from us, looking at us with loving smiles tainted with sadness. After a little while, Dad asked to speak to me outside.

As we sat down in the antiques room, all the questions that had been chasing themselves round my head suddenly spilled out: 'Where's Mum? Is she okay? What's happened?'

Dad took hold of my hands and leaned forward, fixing me with a serious look.

'Your Mum is in jail as she tried to kill me,' he said, very carefully and deliberately. 'She will be standing trial in the next few weeks and I don't know what will happen.'

WHAT? My brain couldn't compute this at all. *My mum tried to kill my dad? No! NO WAY! She wouldn't do that!* I had never known anything but kindness and gentleness from my mother; there wasn't a violent bone in her body. My mind raced but my mouth was frozen. I didn't know where to start!

19

Finally, after a long silence, I spoke: 'Is she okay?'

'She's fine,' Dad replied wearily. He looked tired. 'Dave and Suzie have been to see her and they say she's doing okay.'

'What . . .?' I began, but Dad interrupted me.

'Look, honey, I really can't say much more at the moment. I know this is hard but, trust me, she's fine and I'm going to take us all home today. There's nothing else I can tell you right now.'

I nodded, trying to be brave, trying to be grown-up, but inside, I was distraught.

'What about you, Dad?' I asked. 'Will you be okay?'

'I'll be fine, Tina,' he reassured me. 'One day, I'll explain, but I can't at the minute. I might need an operation in the future but, right now, all you need to know is that I'm okay and we're going home.'

We went home that night with our dad and it was horrible. The house was quiet and pitch-black. I was scared to go in, frightened of seeing that blood again, but Dad didn't hesitate: he marched straight in and flicked the lights on. I crept in slowly behind him – there were no bloodstains on the doorframes. In the living room, the strong smell of gas from the Calor heaters hit me, as did the damp, hot air. The carpets had all been cleaned and the intoxicating smell of chemicals stung my eyes and nose.

I looked around. Everything seemed normal, except the carpet was wet and the huge rug from the middle of the room was missing. Dad went through to the kitchen to make a cup of tea and asked me to get my sisters ready for bed as he was sore and needed to rest.

'Why are you sore, Dad?' I called out. But he didn't answer.

Upstairs in our room, pulling legs and arms through nighties and pyjamas, my curious sisters bombarded me with their questions: where was Mummy? Why wasn't she home?

'Mummy went away to see Granny, down in England,' I lied. 'She'll be back soon.'

I couldn't tell them the truth. How could I? How could I tell my little sisters our wonderful Mum was in jail? We all got into our bed and Dad came through to tuck us in. He was walking strangely and looked as though he was in pain. After kissing us good night, he left. I just lay there, wondering where my Mum was, hoping she was okay.

A few days later, I opened the front door to be met by a dark-haired man with a huge camera around his neck. He could see I was surprised.

'Hello,' he said, too brightly. 'I'm a reporter and would like to talk to your mum or dad, if they are there – it's for a story.'

I had never heard of reporters coming to people's doors, so I was very shocked.

'I'm sorry, there's no one here,' I told him bluntly, suspicious of this man with the too-wide smile. Then he pulled out a card and asked me to give it to one of my parents. When Dad got home an hour later, I told him about the man – he was furious! He said he had been driven mad by reporters and there was going to be a story in the papers the next day. For the next few days, he was keeping us all off school as we might get some problems. I didn't mind – I wasn't in any rush to go to school.

But the next day, when I went to the corner shop to get my penny toffees, the shop owner stopped me.

'Have you seen the paper today?' he asked.

'No, I don't read the papers,' I told him.

'You might want to have a look at today's.'

And so, out of curiosity, and because of the reporter's visit, I bought that day's *Daily Record* and ran home with it under my arm.

Once safe inside the house, I opened it and right there on the inside page was the headline: Unkindest Cut – Beautiful Wife Attacks Husband With Knife. Underneath was a photo of my mum, smiling, her hair flicked back around her fine features, Farrah Fawcett style. It was an old photo Dad had of her – he must have given it to the reporters. It looked so odd, her gorgeous and glamorous picture under such a stark and brutal headline.

I didn't read any more – I just threw down the paper and ran crying to my room. I felt so sick, I didn't know what to do. From the way my dad had been moving and the headline, I put two and two together: Mum had attacked Dad in the private parts. It was horrible. HORRIBLE! I didn't want to know anything more. What was happening to my family? We used to be ordinary people, happy people; now we were appearing in the papers like we were public property and my mum was in jail. Our neighbours would read about Mum and Dad over their morning cups of tea and they would judge and condemn us. *They don't know us!* I was filled with rage. *They don't know anything about our family and our happy years together!* And yet, all that happiness already seemed so far behind us now. How had our lives unravelled so quickly? I didn't understand it at all – nothing made any sense.

I loved my mum, dad and sisters so much but now our home,

our lives and my heart were all broken. At night, while my sisters slept, I cried for hours. It felt like an ocean of tears flooding from my eyes. I wanted so much for all this to be a bad dream but every morning I woke with the same sense of despair and desolation. Why was this happening to us?

Chapter 3

A New Reality

After a few days, Dad sent us all back to school, and now things took a turn for the worse. I was aware of curious eyes sliding over me as I walked into the playground and whispers behind my back in the corridors. One lad who obviously thought he was being funny and brave accosted me in the lunch queue.

'So you're the one whose Mum chopped your Dad's cock off!' he brayed loudly, loud enough for all the kids around us to hear. There were titters behind hands and muffled snorts of laughter.

I couldn't speak. I was so mortified, my face flamed red and I could feel tears welling up behind my eyes. My lip started to quiver and I just put my tray down, turned and walked out of the dining room. The laughter was still ringing in my ears as I slammed into the toilets and bolted the door so I could cry on my own.

By the time lunch was over, I'd more or less pulled myself together but the taunts went on all day long – the sideways glances, the sniggers and the pointing fingers. I'd not been in the school long enough to make any close friends so there was nobody I could confide in, and the teachers didn't make any special effort to talk to me. There was nothing else for it – I just had to pretend everything was okay and push on through.

But inside I was numb. I walked around in a daze, unable to focus on the lessons, the fear of humiliation gripping me tight. My head span, my stomach churned and shame engulfed me like a black cloud. Eventually, in the middle of a maths class, I passed out and was sent home to recover. As my parents weren't around, Maria and Alfonso picked me up to take me home.

There, life was equally bad. Mum still wasn't home and there was nobody to talk to. Dad was now grumpy most of the time, hiding out in the living room, unwilling to communicate or deal with us. It was Gran, his mum, who came over to help out with us girls – but for the most part the parenting now fell to me. I played with the younger ones, got them up and dressed in the morning, took them to school and put them to bed each night with a kiss.

And I missed my mum so much it hurt. I missed the feel of her hugs, the warmth of her exotic scent, the calming, tender voice she used with us children. All the comfort of my home had disappeared and, instead, there was nothing – a terrible emptiness where all the love had once been. Each night, my sisters asked me when Mum was coming home and, automatically, I told them that it was soon, soon, and they weren't to worry. But what did I know? If Mum was found guilty of trying to kill

Dad, we might never see her again. She could be locked away for a very long time.

Each day that went by, I fell further and further into a pit of despair – how could I cope with this? All I wanted was to fall asleep and never wake up again. In desperation, I skipped school one day to go into town, where I bought a strip of aspirin from Boots. I didn't think too hard about dying – I just wanted to end the misery that was engulfing my life. So I gulped down all the eight tablets from the strip and walked to the phone box in the main area of town.

'Hello – the Samaritans,' came the kind voice over the phone. At first, I was too choked to speak, but after a long pause, I cleared my throat and began: 'Hello – I've never done this before but I'm feeling really bad and I don't want to live any more.'

'It's okay,' the voice said. It belonged to a woman, and her calm, caring tone reminded me of my mother. I missed her so much at that moment I wanted to scream out. The woman waited a little and then she went on: 'My name is Sonya and I'm here for when you feel able to talk.'

After swallowing hard, I told the lady that I had just taken some aspirin and I wanted to die.

'Everything has gone wrong at home and I don't think I can cope,' I told her as I wiped the tears from my cheeks. I burbled on, telling her about my mum hurting my dad and Mum being in jail. I poured out my feelings to the stranger on the other end of the phone. It was such a relief to tell someone what was going on and all my fears and thoughts about being a bad daughter and how I blamed myself.

'Tina, none of this is your fault and though I know you

are going through a very hard time right now, things will get better,' Sonya said. 'There isn't anything in life worth ending your own life for.'

Her words made me feel a little better and after I got everything off my chest I realised I didn't want to die any more. So I went back along to Boots and asked if they had a sick bay – by now I was feeling woozy and my head was spinning again. I was frightened I might actually die but I lay down on their little bed and slept. It was a great sleep with no worries. They woke me up at five as the shop was closing and I walked home. Once inside, I went straight to bed. Dad didn't even seem to notice that I was back. Thankfully, I hadn't taken enough aspirin to do me any harm.

I waited, day after day, but nothing seemed to get any better and knowing now that I didn't want to die, I felt I had to at least get out of the house. So I found the number of our local orphanage in the phone book and called them.

'Hello – my name is Tina and I need to come in,' I told them frankly. 'I'm very unhappy at home – a lot of terrible things have happened recently and I need somewhere safe to live.'

Even as I was speaking the guilt at leaving behind my three sisters to cope alone weighed heavily on my shoulders. But right now I just needed to escape. The reaction was not what I was expecting. A harsh little chortle echoed down the line.

'Don't be so ridiculous, Tina!' the woman admonished sternly. 'You can't just come in because you're feeling a bit low – it doesn't work like that! Stay at home and sort things out with your family. We can't help. Goodbye.'

The line at the other end went dead and, for a moment, I just stood there, staring dumbly at the receiver. The woman had been so callous and uncaring. I had reached out to somebody, I had asked for help, and yet I was turned away with a laugh. It made me feel even smaller and more insignificant than I did already.

So the overwhelming sense of sadness simply stayed with me while I carried out my duties at home with increasing lethargy. After four weeks, I came home from school one day and immediately sensed a change. Dad looked agitated and tense, but I could smell the familiar scent of Cinnabar: Mum!

I ran through to the kitchen and there, seated opposite the door at the cream Formica breakfast bar was my mum, her delicate hands wrapped around a cup of tea. It was wonderful to see her and I fell into her arms, cherishing the first hug in a whole month. But as I pulled away, I saw a very strange look in her eye. Gone was the bright, easy smile, the carefree glamour – now I saw a woman overcome with shock, shame and misery. She was wearing the blue wrap-around dress that flattered her tall, curvy figure, but there was something missing from her face. Even as my sisters covered her in hugs and kisses, I saw her expression was flat and vacant.

'How did court go?' I asked her, breathless with the excitement at her return.

'Fine,' she replied. 'I won.' And that was all I needed to hear – I'd been so frightened that Mum would go to jail for ever and we'd never see her again. At last, the fear I'd been carrying round all these weeks disappeared in an instant. But to my surprise, instead of the happiness I was expecting, I was suddenly consumed with anger. White, hot burning rage – at her, my mother!

A voice inside my head erupted and the words I heard were so vicious and nasty, I felt utter shame for thinking them: *It's all her fault! She's caused all of this. She hurt your dad, she went to prison, she split up your family, she caused you all nothing but misery and now look at her, just sitting here, not saying anything! She hasn't even said sorry! She's not sorry. All she cares about is herself. She doesn't care about any of us or she wouldn't have done it to start with!*

The feelings were sudden, ferocious and made me instantly guilty. I couldn't look at my mum then; I could barely speak to her. It was horrible to hate her so much but, at that moment, it was all I could feel. I wanted her to reach out to all of us and apologise and promise to make it right; I wanted her to love Dad again. But without us realising, Dad had slipped out of the house during our reunion with Mum. And he didn't come back. For the next few days, we were off school to spend time with Mum but something definitely wasn't right: she didn't laugh any more, she didn't even smile. Her skin and eyes were dull.

On top of that, our whole routine had gone. There were no more family dinners, sat round the table together, talking and catching up on the day. No more delicious pasta dishes or roast lunches followed by Mum's legendary baked Alaska. Now she just knocked up something quick and cheap for tea – like fish fingers and chips – and left it on the table for us to have when we wanted. Then she'd go through to the living room to watch TV or even disappear into her bedroom, where she shut the door.

A week later, I was back at school but as miserable and paranoid as before. It felt like everyone was looking at me and laughing – I couldn't concentrate in my lessons so there didn't seem to be any point being there any more. On the third day back, I bunked off. I would never have thought of doing something like this before but now it seemed the only solution to my anxiety. I sat in the park on my own and watched the mothers chasing their toddlers across the playground. They seemed happy.

My school absence didn't seem to matter – at home, Mum had stopped bothering to check our homework or read with us. Katie and Sophie just watched TV or fought. Mum didn't even notice when they were punching lumps out of each other. The screaming and yelling washed right over her and she put herself to bed earlier and earlier each night. In the mornings, she didn't bother getting up either, leaving us all to sort out our own breakfast and get our school uniforms on.

I was in the Wellgate shopping centre one day, bunking off school, when I bumped into Diane, my good friend from Africa. I could not believe it. She told me when her family left Africa, they came back to Dundee and her school had a swimming pool – and that was it for me! Well, I was sold – I missed swimming more than anything else. We spent the next hour in the Wellgate with her friends, who were all lovely and I felt like I just fitted in with them. It gave me a happy feeling seeing Diane again and I rushed home to tell Mum I wanted to go to Diane's school. I thought it would be the answer to my prayers: swimming would make me happy again and perhaps I could get back to dancing, especially ballet and gymnastics, which I also loved.

Mum said she would sort it out for me then walked back to

her room, smoking. She had always smoked but, before, she held herself so well it looked elegant and grown-up. Now she sucked greedily on each cigarette with long draws and her hunched shoulders and absent expression made her look sad and desperate. She said Dad had gone to live somewhere else but he would see us all again soon and a couple of weeks later she announced that he would meet all us girls in the Wellgate shopping centre.

We were excited to see him again – we were lacking any parenting at all right then and needed his safe, secure arms. But as the hours slid slowly by and Dad failed to arrive at our pre-arranged meeting spot on the bench, my heart swelled with sadness. Where was he? Didn't he care about us either? Week after week, we went to our spot in the Wellgate and, more often than not, waited alone and pointlessly for our dad, who didn't show up. I wanted to feel sorry for him; after all, he was the one who had been hurt. But it was hard to understand why he didn't come and see us.

One night after school, he surprised us by turning up at the house after tea. He and Mum gave each other a hard stare then Mum beckoned me into the living room while the others finished off their tea of Findus Crispy Pancakes. I'd already rejected mine – I hated them!

Mum was sitting patiently on the sofa when I came in and Dad was sat next to her, but they might as well have been in different rooms. The distance between them was palpable.

'Tina, we have to tell you something,' she started. 'We need to sell the house. We're moving and fast. The house is about to be repossessed so I need to find somewhere else quick or we will be homeless.'

That was all she said. At this point, I was so traumatised by everything I couldn't make sense of her words. Everything was such a mess already and now she was telling me we were going to be homeless? Dad looked down at his hands, a guilty expression on his face. Mum seemed angry – her words were tense and sparse.

'When?' I asked.

'Soon,' she responded quickly. 'But we'll get something else. I just want you to know that it won't be long.'

I got up and walked out of the room. It felt like our lives were in freefall – now our beautiful home was going. I loved our house! I loved the view over the big, grassy field, where I would dream of one day having my own horse; I loved our bedroom with all the toys and space; I loved our modern kitchen with the breakfast bar and large radiator that made it so warm, even when it was freezing cold outside. My perfect life was being scrubbed away with a dirty rag – I felt worthless.

Half an hour later, after Dad left, Mum took me aside and, in a low, urgent whisper, the whole thing came tumbling out.

'It's your father's fault!' she hissed. 'He's in debt – right up to his ears! I thought he'd been paying the bills for the shop, the house and the business, but he hasn't. There's nothing left. I have to sell the shop, too. You didn't know this but all the bills that have been coming in – well, he's been hiding them from me. And he's been using your sisters to hide them, too. Can you imagine? The bastard! I had no idea. *No* idea! There's other stuff, too – but I won't go into it now. Trust me, this is just the tip of the iceberg. Tina, we have to leave here because your father has been lying to us all.'

Through all of this, I was silent – I wanted to respond but I didn't know how. It was too much to take in.

As preparations were made for us to leave, Dad sometimes turned up to help get rid of the stuff. It all had to be sold to help pay the debts. And it was heart-breaking, watching our lives being dismantled, piece by piece – out went the Chesterfield, the fireguards, chairs, wardrobes, wooden bureau and green chaise longue. My heart sank whenever I saw him in the house, knowing that eventually the shouting would start.

It never took long.

'Go on! Take the bloody stereo, you lying bastard!' I'd hear my mum shriek as they fought over every bit of furniture. 'I don't bloody care! You've taken everything else!'

'Please, Lucy, not in front of the children . . .' Dad would plead.

'Oh, yes, that's right: the *children*! *Now* you care about the children, *now* you give a shit about what's best for them! You didn't care about that before, did you? Didn't think about our family when you were off sleeping with that . . .'

'Lucy, stop!'

'You're a lying bastard, a cheater and a bloody loser! Look what you've done, you've destroyed us! So much for your love – you don't love any of us! Are you happy now? *Well?* ARE YOU?'

'For God's sake, Lucy! I'm leaving.'

'Yes, walk away, why don't you? Walk away – that's what you're good at!'

The ferocity of these outbursts was too much for me. I tried to shield my sisters from them by leading them into our bedroom to play; where we'd put on our cassettes to try to drown out the hurtful words but the shouts thudded through the walls, stabbing at our already bruised little hearts. They used to love each other so much and I couldn't understand where all that love had gone.

One day, Dad came round and he put his Neil Diamond record on my stereo. I guess I was angry with him now because I just walked up to the record player, took it off and replaced it with my 7-inch single of Madness's 'The Sun And The Rain'. I was stood in front of the record when he came through and yelled at me: 'Get that off!'

Turning to him defiantly, I replied: 'No.'

I had never spoken back to my dad before and he stormed up to me, pushed me out of the way, tore my precious record off the player and threw it out of the window. I stood there, stunned, as I watched him run over to the coffee table, pick up Mum's beautiful teapot that she cherished and fling it against the wall, smashing it into a million little pieces.

I was shocked but at the same time determined he wasn't going to get away with it so, after he stormed out, I grabbed all of his records and hid them. Then I ran off out of the house and sat in the park until late at night, too scared to go home. Until that moment, I'd never talked back to my parents but now everything was in turmoil and I was terrified of what he'd do when I got home. So I sat there in the dark, looking out over the park lit up with the streetlights, and feeling very, very lonely. I went back eventually and Mum was there. When I told her about the fight, she just hugged me and told me to go to bed, saying everything would be okay.

But it only seemed to get worse. Before we left the house for good, Mum was offered a flat in a homeless unit. We walked for miles to see it and when we arrived, I wished we hadn't bothered. The depressing tower block was covered in graffiti; windows were blocked with metal sheets and drunk, scary-looking men hung out at the entrance. I grabbed Mum's hand as we walked in and my nostrils were immediately filled with the unmistakable stench of urine. Inside the dark stone corridor, it was freezing, cold and damp. *What was that on the walls?* I wondered as we took the staircase, two steps at a time. *It looked like shit. But it couldn't be, could it?*

Mum's steps sped up, her breathing grew heavier, and by the time we reached the right floor, she practically ran inside the flat, pulling us all in with such force. If it were possible, the flat was even worse on the inside. The carpets, where there were any, were filthy, the wallpaper was peeling off the walls, exposing bare brick, and the whole place smelled rotten and disgusting. Mum started to cry and we all ran to hug her.

This was a nightmare, a real nightmare.

Chapter 4

The Truth

Mum gazed out of the window and let out a deep sigh. She was curled up on the sofa under a thick tartan blanket and smoke from her lit cigarette snaked delicately up towards the ceiling. In the twilight, her face was a mask of misery. I hated to see her like this.

In the end, she refused to take the homeless unit – it was just too horrible – and instead, we moved to a tiny council one-bedroom flat; but with the debts and the loss of the business, money was now a serious problem. We had no money to run the electric so, as night time crept in earlier and earlier, we got used to living in darkness. Not only were there times when we had no electric, but we could never afford to put the hot water on and had to wash in freezing water. Shampoo was a luxury we could barely afford and would either use a bar of soap or washing up liquid to wash our hair, which became matted.

Toilet roll was also something that was classed as a luxury and we often had to use newspaper. We were so ashamed of the way our lives had become and felt very degraded and small. It was depressing enough but occasionally Mum would mutter to herself: 'Where is he now? I bet your dad is out having fun. And look at us, sat here with nothing!'

The worst thing was, she was right. On the rare occasions we did see Dad, he was full of beans, thrilled at his newfound freedom. He'd tell us about the nights he'd go out clubbing, meeting new women, hooking up with old friends. It was lovely to see him so happy but it ate me up inside, knowing he was putting us through this.

The one good thing in my life was that shortly after the move, Mum got me into Whitfield High School, where my friend Diane was a pupil. I started swimming again and did dance and gymnastics classes, which made me feel alive. At Whitfield, I slotted easily into Diane's circle of friends and for the first time in a long while, I felt happy and accepted among my peers. Of course, it didn't stop the whispers in the corridor or the intrusive stares, but at least now I had friends I could have fun with.

In truth, everyone in my group was in the same boat. Most were from broken homes, and many lived on the breadline. We didn't talk about it because there didn't seem much point, but going home each night was torture.

Some days there wasn't enough for food so us girls were sent to the shop to buy chips with the bottles we had saved up. Each empty bottle was worth a few pence – we scavenged in the bins behind people's houses and though it was humiliating, walking up to the shop with all our bottles clanking around, it was better than going hungry. The kids who hung round there would snigger at us and I'd hide my face with embarrassment. I didn't see the funny side at all.

Some days I simply refused food just to make sure my sisters had something on their plates. At school we got free lunch tickets that were a lifesaver because sometimes it was our only meal of the day. But as time went on and I started to smoke and rebel, I'd sell my tickets for cash to buy cigarettes or a Diet Pepsi. Mum was in her own world of depression and slept a lot when she was not working. She had no energy to challenge us four at all.

On top of that, I had huge holes in the bottom and sides of my shoes and we could not afford new ones. I'd stand with my feet together just so no one would see. I hated living like this, as did my sisters. By now they were completely out of control. Mum was so absent most of the time – either sleeping or working one of her part-time bar jobs to try to make ends meet – that Katie and Sophie ran wild with their friends, smashing windows, pulling washing off lines, smoking and generally getting up to no good. There were times I came to blows with Katie because she had such a temper. She was full of anger. Sophie was much quieter, but equally out of control. Celine was too young to be doing anything so she was always in the house. I would just sit with her when I could and hug her. I knew how I felt – God only knows how they coped!

Life went on in this way for the next two years – a desperate struggle to survive in a dark and cold world. I began to feel numb. The only love I felt was for my sisters. I felt completely cut off from my mum and dad.

I slipped deeper into a state of crushing misery. All the positivity in my head was now replaced by bleakness and negative thoughts. The happy, bubbly, loving girl I'd once been was gone. It was as if a stranger had moved into my head and that stranger did not like me at all. The new person in my head wanted to be alone, fearful no one would want to be in my company anyway. *Why would they?* It sneered meanly. *After all, you are stupid, ugly, smelly, poor and retarded!*

The only thing that made me feel good about myself was exercise — it made me feel special in a strange way. I could not talk to anyone about my feelings and even though my mum tried to make us feel comfortable about being open, we were reticent children. None of us talked about the divorce or our descent into poverty, we were all so deeply ashamed of what had happened. We didn't talk about the friends who weren't allowed to play at our house because their parents thought my mum was a monster, or the people who stared at us, or joked at our expense.

One night, I'd finally had enough. After the years of silence, I wanted to know the truth — I was tired of being angry with my parents, tired of keeping all my questions to myself. So that evening, after the others had gone to bed, I sat down next to Mum in our tiny lounge and, summoning all my strength, I asked her: 'Why did you hurt Dad?'

Her blue eyes fell on me then as if seeing me for the first time. She took a drag of her cigarette and said: 'I wondered when you were going to ask.'

There was a silence then and I waited. Mum sighed heavily, pulled the rug up around her knees and looked down at her hands. I waited to hear the truth.

'You know before *it* happened we went to your grandma's house in England?' she started. I nodded. 'You remember Dad stayed here because he had to work? Well, something happened in those two weeks – he met a woman. It was nothing in particular that gave it away and yet to me, I knew instantly there was something wrong. There was the time I called the house and he wasn't there. A time he really should have been home. Another time I called and he was talking strangely so I just knew, I knew something wasn't right.

'I confronted him when we got back and your father, well, he didn't deny it – quite the opposite, in fact!' She laughed bitterly. 'He told me everything in graphic detail, didn't leave anything out. He'd met this young woman – young and hot, he'd called her – and she'd flirted with him. He lapped it up and they started seeing each other – dinners, long walks, romantic trysts. It was a fling, yes, but the way he talked about her – his eyes lit up, he was so excited!

'Of course, I was devastated, hurt beyond belief. Tina, I had no idea there was anything wrong with our marriage. I didn't know he was unhappy. As far as I was concerned, we had a happy, strong marriage, a wonderful home, great businesses. It never even occurred to me he'd do anything so destructive.'

Now Mum was crying silently and she let the tears fall into her lap.

'I was hysterical; I couldn't cope. Dad was upset, too – he didn't want the marriage to end. He loved me, he said, he knew he'd fucked up big time with his selfish actions, ruined our lives. But I don't think he understood just how much he'd hurt me. It was unbearable.'

Finally, things were making sense. I could see even now my mum found it difficult to talk about this – Dad had broken her heart.

'There was no going back,' she went on. 'He couldn't change what he'd done. Not only that but he confessed about the debt as well. I don't know what had happened to him. He'd got into trouble so quickly after we started the businesses but he didn't tell me about it. If only he'd come to me, if only he'd shared his problems, we could have tried to fix it together, but it got so bad that by the time he told me, it was over. I lost the business, the house, everything! Well, after that, it was too much – the lies, the deception. It was the death of all my dreams.

'I lay awake night after night, sobbing, imagining your father with this other woman. I couldn't get the images out of my head! I felt so humiliated, Tina. And I just wanted him to be humiliated in the same way. I couldn't eat, couldn't sleep, my insides ached all the time with anger and the only thing I thought would help ease it would be by hurting him back. It was the darkest time of my life and I suppose something slipped in my mind. I lost my sense and I decided he had to pay for his actions.'

Looking back now it was strange to think of my parents utterly miserable and us completely unaware. They hid it so well, just carrying on as normal, not raising their voices or losing their tempers in front of us.

'So that's when I came up with my idea,' she went on. 'One night I told him I was thinking perhaps we could get back together. I asked him to come into the lounge to talk to me about it after you kids had gone to bed. I knew this was the night so I hid a sharp, black-handled knife under the rug in the lounge. We talked for about an hour – don't ask me what we talked about; I can't, for the life of me, remember and I was too hyped up to concentrate on what he was saying anyway. I felt scared, nervous and mad all at the same time.

'Anyway, we lay on the rug together and I made him think that I was feeling amorous towards him so he let me undo his trouser buttons. Then I took the knife out and cut across the top of his penis – I cut right through so it was just hanging on with some skin, vein and sinew. He let out this blood-curdling scream of agony and at that moment I felt this strange sense of calm settle on me.

'I said to him: "That's what you get for wrecking our lives, you selfish bastard!" Then I just walked off, calm as you like. I didn't think it would kill him – I'd done a bit of research – so I just felt very serene. He was screaming and desperately trying to get into the hallway to call for help from the phone but I was in another world by now. I walked through to the kitchen, washed my hands and made myself a cup of tea. I could hear Dad in the lounge, crying in pain, but I just left him.

'I swear, Tina, I must have lost it by then because I felt so calm – it was as if I was in a dream-state. Nothing felt real but, for the first time in a fortnight, my heart was at peace. The ambulance arrived and shortly afterwards the police came and took me away in handcuffs.'

I was stunned. The way Mum was describing it seemed she had truly lost her mind. Suddenly, something occurred to me.

'The screams,' I said, 'why didn't we hear the screams and wake up?'

'I made sure all the doors were shut,' she explained simply. 'I didn't want to disturb you girls, didn't want you to have to suffer.'

I nearly laughed then. She had been so careful not to frighten us and yet the whole thing had been terrifying nonetheless. I wondered if she ever thought about the impact this had had on us.

Mum went on: 'They charged me with attempted murder and at first I didn't mind. I wanted to be in jail, actually – I think I needed the rest, mentally. Obviously, I had had some kind of breakdown. My mind had gone somewhere else and I wasn't at all myself. Funnily enough, when the other women inmates found out about what I'd done, I got lots of pats on the back. Many even told me they would have done the same. I didn't care – actually, I didn't really notice the others too much. I just lay in the cell every day, thinking about the future and what we were going to do. I spoke to a few psychiatrists while I was there and that definitely helped.

'I got a visit from Suzie and Dave and they said that you girls were doing okay and they also said Dad was out of hospital. He wasn't interested in pressing charges, apparently, but this was a criminal matter and the decision wasn't his to make. Fortunately, I had a wonderful lawyer – she advised me to plead guilty with diminished responsibility because of the mental breakdown, which I did. And when it went before the court, the judge said that, under the circumstances, I would be admonished of all charges, which basically meant I got off.

'As relieved as I felt that I wouldn't be in jail for life, it was actually a bit sad to leave all the lovely people I met in prison.

Prison is a great leveller, Tina. There are many reasons people end up there – either by circumstance or choice. I don't think anyone can ever say they won't end up in jail – you just don't know what's around the corner.'

All this time, as Mum was telling her story, I'd been sat opposite her in complete shock. It was a strange enough story for real life, let alone your own mother's life! Of course, everything made sense now – the reason Mum had been so destroyed after she came back, Dad's pain, the sniggers from the schoolyard. I even recalled that a few days before the event, Mum had stood over me while I was doing my biology homework and looked at the diagrams of the male reproductive system. I felt suddenly guilty that she had got her information from my books! It was too much – I really didn't want to hear any more.

'Erm, right,' I mumbled, squirming with discomfort. 'Well, thanks – I'm going to bed now.'

That night, I cried for a long time into my pillow. I cried for my mum and the death of her dreams, for the violent end to their marriage, for my dad's desperate and secret struggles with debt, and for all the years of poverty and unhappiness we had suffered up till now. But most of all, I cried for myself – I cried for the end of my childhood, the end of my innocence.

Chapter 5

Sliding

'**J**esus Christ!' I exclaimed as the toxic fumes stung my eyes. It felt like my throat was on fire. I looked down into the bag of Evo-Stik glue from which I'd just inhaled and, for a moment, the world started to spin. Then a funny buzzing sound started up in my head and my teeth clamped together involuntarily.

'Fuck me!' I whispered to myself. All alone in the Pavilion on Baxter Park, I had decided to try glue sniffing for the first time. Usually, I hung around here with my pals but because this was my first time, I didn't want to do it in front of the others in case I ended up making a tit of myself. But not really knowing how to do it properly, I'd emptied the whole tube into the plastic bag and inhaled a huge lungful of fumes. *Ah, well, in for a penny, in for a pound*, I thought. I stuck my head back in the bag and sucked up another big lungful. Then I passed out.

The next thing I knew, I was waking up on the cold concrete

floor of the Pavilion, my head pounding, hands still gripping the bag of glue. It was now pitch-black.

Oh, my God, how long have I been unconscious for?

I remembered coming to the park in the early evening but now it looked like it was really late. I staggered to my feet and tried to walk home but I was drunk on fumes, my head was fuzzy and I felt very odd. When I touched my face, which was numb, my fingers came to rest on patches of hardened glue stuck to my cheeks. So as I swerved and stumbled back home, I tried to pick the glue off.

It was like walking in a dream – without being able to feel my legs, I seemed to float. I just had to trust to instinct that I was actually managing to put one foot in front of the other.

Shit! I giggled manically to myself. *I'm really wasted!* But the best thing of all was that I felt absolutely numb inside. No sadness, no bad thoughts; no stranger telling me I was crap and unworthy – the glue had effectively chased out all my demons. I walked into the house, went straight to bed and fell fast asleep. When I woke up the next morning, I felt terrible. There was a huge lump on my forehead, which must have happened when I passed out and fell off the bench. By the time I left for school, Mum was still in bed. *Oh, well.* I shrugged. *She probably wouldn't notice anyway and definitely wouldn't care.*

Now I spent all my time with my new friends, walking around the streets of Dundee, getting drunk, smoking joints, sniffing glue and having a laugh. None of us had money, so we would put our pennies together to buy cigarettes and cheap cider. I didn't talk about my home life to anyone – my shame silenced me and, in any case, bringing up the subject of my mum and dad invited horrible feelings that I simply didn't want to deal with any more. No, all I wanted to do was get really, really plastered so I didn't have to think or feel.

I cut myself off from my family and though most of the time Mum wasn't around, there was the occasional showdown when she'd pull me up about my late nights, roving around town. One night, I got in drunk and late, my hair a mess and my face studded with glue as usual, and she was standing in the hallway, ready to give me hell.

'Do you know what time it is?' she hissed, hands anchored on her hips, eyes blazing. I ignored her, pushing past her to get to my room, too pissed to care.

'It's *midnight*! Tina, this is unacceptable. You're not eighteen, you are fifteen years old and you have school tomorrow.'

'Ah, shove it!' I whispered under my breath.

'You're not getting away with this,' she carried on, following me to my room. I tried to close the door behind me but she put her foot in the doorway, to stop me.

'You're grounded – for two weeks!' she dropped her voice low since my sisters were asleep, just feet away. And at that, I laughed out loud. Grounded? As if! She couldn't ground me, she couldn't do *anything*!

Of course, she did try. After I got home from school the next day, she locked the front door and hid the key. But I wasn't going to take this from her. What did she care what I did? It wasn't her decision. I just opened the kitchen window, climbed out and slid down the drainpipe. As far as I was concerned, my mum had no control over me any more. Working all her many jobs meant she was barely there in person and when she was around, she was so completely absent in every other way she didn't seem to notice what was going on. In my mind, she had effectively checked out of motherhood years before so I didn't see why I had to do as she said.

I tried everything that year – I just wanted to escape into oblivion and sometimes I did that so effectively I passed out for hours. One time, I tried sniffing aerosol spray. My friends had a can of butane gas. They took the little nozzle off and pressed it into a cloth really hard. Once the cloth went hard and cold, they started inhaling and sucking the fumes through their mouth and nose. Thinking it looked really easy, I had a go, too.

It floored me on my first small breath. There was an intense buzzing sound in my head. My sight disappeared completely and my whole face started to tingle with pins and needles. It was horrible and, for the first time, I was actually quite frightened. For a few minutes, I was unable to move or speak. Eventually, I came back to normal but I felt terrible afterwards and never touched it again.

At school, I was sliding even further behind in my studies. I'd been put in all the lowest sets, so it felt like I really was as thick as I imagined. In frustration, I took out my anger on my teachers, talking back to them and being rude. I didn't have any respect left – for myself or anyone else. Even getting the belt didn't stop me giving them mouth. I'd tell them to fuck off or refuse their requests for homework.

I thought none of my teachers noticed that I was getting out of control but there was one. It was the last class of the day and Mr Findlay, my maths teacher, asked me to stay behind after the bell went. As the chairs scraped along the floor and the other kids battled boisterously to get out of the door, I shoved my books in my bag and gave Mr Findlay short shrift. After all, I had plans that afternoon – plans to drink in the park with my mates.

'No, sorry,' I said dismissively, not even looking at him. 'I'm far too busy and, anyway, you can't make me.'

But Mr Findlay wasn't going to take no for an answer. He put his hand on my bag and looked directly at me.

'This is very important, Tina,' he said seriously. 'It's about going forward with maths.' I could tell from his tone he wasn't messing around. Mr Findlay was a youngish teacher, in his mid-thirties, who wore steel-framed glasses and slouchy trousers. He wasn't exactly cool but then he wasn't an old duffer either. Occasionally, he could make the class laugh, which was saying something among our group of hard nuts, each with his own brand of bad attitude.

'Fine,' I stropped, flouncing back in my seat and refusing to meet his eye. I suppose I didn't have any choice – I had to listen to him harangue me about my work, wasting both our time! I knew as well as he did that I was on course to flunk the year. As the last of the pupils made it out of the classroom, Mr Findlay closed the door behind them and came to sit on the desk in front of me. For a while, he didn't say anything, just looked at me, his brow creased with concern. So I stared back at him haughtily.

'Look, Tina – I just want to know: are you okay?'

I was shocked. For a minute, my couldn't-give-a-shit attitude slipped and my heart began to thump. I didn't think anyone had noticed what was going on but it seemed one person had! The question was so open and genuine, as if he could see straight through my cool-as-you-like attitude to the scared little girl underneath. Undone, I felt exposed and vulnerable. For a moment, I didn't know what to say.

I had two choices, either lie and say everything was okay or spill the beans about my pathetic life and how I'd let everything get so out of control. I needed help, and fast. But I couldn't just let this teacher into my inner world so easily – after all, I'd spent a long while building up my outer defences. Who was he to think he could just break them all down with one little question?

'Yes, of course I'm fine,' I lied, smiling sweetly. 'Why?'

'Yellow Belly,' he challenged me gently, pointing at the bright yellow tank top I was wearing over my white shirt. 'I don't believe you – you don't seem fine to me.'

This was way too much – his kindness and concern was beginning to get to me and I just wanted out. I couldn't cope and I didn't see how he could change things anyway. So I just pushed myself up, grabbed my bag and walked out, still smiling, but now fighting down the tears. As I got to the door, I turned back briefly and gave a half-hearted little wave: 'It's all good, Mr Findlay.' Then I left.

He must have known I was lying – I really wasn't a very good liar – and as I walked slowly down the corridor that afternoon, my emotions bubbled up inside me. It was nice to know someone cared and, deep down, all I really wanted to do was run back in there and ask him for a massive hug, then open my heart to him. I wanted to ask him for help to make my life better, but I couldn't. I just didn't know how. Instead, I kept walking – walking towards my destructive destiny.

Things didn't get any better after that. I stopped telling my mum about parents' evenings – I didn't want it confirmed to her what I already knew: that I was stupid and failing in all my subjects. In any case, I had other things on my mind. I decided to join my friends in getting tattoos. I got my name tattooed on my left forearm, next to my elbow, and 'YWS' tattooed on my right forearm, the initials for the Young Whitfield Shams, the gang I wanted to become part of. At home, I wore long-sleeved tops so my family wouldn't see. On top of that, I had my whole head shaved, except for a flick of hair at the front, and I got nine piercings in my ears– just to be different!

I also started experimenting with make-up, caking my face in thick foundation and drawing on dark eyebrows with a black kohl pencil. I felt ugly, inside and out, so I just wanted to hide from the world. My insecurities were now so bad, I didn't even like to look people in the eye.

There were only two good things in my life at this point: my contemporary dance classes, which I went to whenever I had enough money from working at the chip shop or selling my dinner ticket, and my boyfriend, Jack. The dancing was something that always made me feel good about myself. Flying through the air, doing back flips and the splits, gave me a rare sense of freedom and, for a few hours a week, I felt truly happy and alive. I was able to get away from all my unhappiness and silence the voice in my head that never seemed to leave me alone now.

Jack, my new boyfriend, was a nice distraction, too. He was Dave's younger brother and we'd met at the fish-and-chip shop one day when I was serving. He was a couple of years older than me and so handsome and tall at 6 ft 2 inches. He'd asked me out to the movies one night and from there we started seeing each other. Jack was a very sweet boy and he really seemed to adore me, even when I cut off all my hair, got tattoos and pierced my ears. I loved him, too, but it was hard to fight down my insecurities when I was around him. Though he was always kind and considerate, I feared it wouldn't last. *He'll stop loving you one day*, said the cruel voice in my head, *you're just not good enough for him.*

For the summer I turned sixteen, I was taken on my first foreign holiday. It was Maria and Alfonso's idea. Their whole family – including Suzie, Dave and their two young children – was going to Italy for a couple of months, to see relatives, and I think they must have seen I needed a little time out. They had asked my parents some months before if I wanted to join them and I'd jumped at the opportunity, so now all my wages from working in the fish-and-chip shop went towards my spending money for the trip.

As I waved goodbye to my sisters that sunny day in June 1985, my heart fluttered with excitement, tinged with anxiety. It was the first time I had left them for any length of time and I worried if they'd be okay without me, especially Celine as we were so close. But as the miles slid behind us and we drove out of Dundee, caught the ferry and crossed into Europe, my senses were filled with new sights, smells, sounds and experiences. It was amazing!

At first, we drove to France, where we stayed with their friends for a few days, before going through Switzerland and then on to Italy. We stayed in Rimini and made day trips to

San Marino and other pretty towns and villages. The family looked after me as if I was one of their own and the food was always excellent, wherever we went. There was a café below the apartment and they sold the best, thickest hot chocolate I had ever had in my life. I simply had to have one every day! We spent weeks hanging out on Rimini beach and, at first, it was wonderful but then one day, something happened that changed my life for ever.

It was early morning and already the beach was alive with throngs of holidaymakers. There were loungers and people everywhere you looked, talking, playing games, laughing or simply sunbathing. I had been in the sea in my red all-in-one swimsuit and was standing on the sand, letting the sun dry me off, when I turned around.

In that second, I saw two women lying on a lounger next to me, and it appeared one of them was gesturing towards me, her hands open wide, as if indicating something was very big. In that split second, I was filled with horror. *Oh, my God, it's me! She's saying my backside looks huge!*

Until that moment, I'd never worried about my figure. I danced, swam and did gymnastics, so I always assumed I was quite fit and healthy. But now it felt like a switch was going off in my head and the voice inside started shouting at me: *You are fucking huge! You are a whale! You are massive. MASSIVE! It's embarrassing! Look at yourself!*

I had to get away; I had to do something about it. So I threw on my sundress and ran back to our apartment, where I locked myself in the toilet. Then I stuck my fingers down my throat and threw up the breakfast and juice I'd eaten not long before. I just felt that I had to get the food out of my body as quickly as possible and it occurred to me that I could do this by throwing up. Then, when I'd finished, I went to stand in front of the full-length mirror in my room. Now, instead of being content with my body, I was filled with horror. How could I not have noticed this before? How had I let things get so out of control? It was like my eyes had opened for the first time and at last I could truly see what I'd become.

Holly shit, Tina, you look like an elephant! The voice inside my head boomed. *Look at those massive thunder thighs, and that fat massive arse, and, even worse, the arms!* I was repulsed by my reflection. How had I let myself get to such an enormous size? I had to do something about it right away.

So for the rest of that holiday, I enjoyed the great food as usual with the family, but afterwards, I excused myself to go to the toilet, where I made myself sick to get rid of what I'd just eaten. Anything was better than getting fat! I hid this, of course, from Maria, Alfonso and the others – I didn't want them to see the lengths I had to go to in order to slim down. In my mind, I really was a disgusting pig.

This became my daily habit – eating then running to a toilet to throw up. If I couldn't do that, I'd just take a small bite of my food, chew it a while, then spit it out into a tissue under the table. Almost overnight, my eating habits had changed and I knew I had to stick to the new rules or I'd never be happy again.

After two months in Italy, during which I turned sixteen, we made the long drive home. I was sad to leave – it was a fantastic place, with great culture, food and people – but I had gone to Italy a normal healthy girl and come back a completely different person. Now my life took on a whole new purpose and I was ready for the challenge ahead . . .

Chapter 6

The Best Anorexic
in the World

121. Push! 122. Push! 123. Must push harder! Every fibre in my stomach muscles screamed out in pain and the sweat dribbled down my temples as I counted the sit-ups, hands locked behind my head. I couldn't stop now – I HAD to get to my target of 150 before I could allow myself to rest, so I sucked in my stomach, scrunched up my face against the burning in my abdomen and pushed myself on. *124. Yes! 125. Keep going! MUST. KEEP. GOING!*

When I hit my target number, I collapsed back onto my bedroom floor, my head swimming, chest heaving, yet filled with a huge sense of satisfaction. I grinned to myself: I'd beaten yesterday's target of 130 by 20 sit-ups and now I could take a short break before starting on the 200 star jumps in my regime.

Exercise had become my new best friend. Since returning from Italy, life at home was as depressing as ever. Mum was hardly ever around but now I had a new reason to stay in and not go out with my mates: I had to shift this disgusting fat that I would squeeze with my hands every night. It wasn't hard to ditch the friends – all I had to do was stop going out. After all, alcohol was fattening so I couldn't allow myself to get drunk any more.

Each night, I went to my room and started a routine of exercise that gradually became more and more testing. At first, I was just doing 50 sit-ups, 50 squats, 50 push-ups, running on the spot for 10 minutes and doing 50 star jumps. But every day, I increased my target numbers and it always gave me a huge rush when I pushed myself to my limits. Exercise was something I was actually really good at and knowing I was burning up all that horrible fat made me feel I was accomplishing something.

I was 5 ft 5 inches and started out at 9 stone. When I looked in the mirror I felt physically sick. *If people see you like this they'll be repulsed!* the voice in my head told me. *You are fat, ugly and worthless.* The only way to beat the voice was to exercise non-stop – so any time I went anywhere, I ran. I sprinted to school, ran home, ran to the shop and I even ran over the bridge at night to see Jack.

Food was now an uncomfortable issue. I didn't like people watching me eat any more – the voice told me that I looked like a 'greedy fat pig' whenever I ate so, even in front of my sisters, I hid my mouth behind my hand when I was eating. Even so, with every little nibble, the voice repeated over and over: *Greedy fat pig, greedy fat pig, greedy fat pig!*

After a few weeks, I could see a change in my body and Jack too noticed I was getting slimmer.

'God, look at the gap between your waist and your jeans! They're hanging off you,' he exclaimed one night as I sprawled out on his large bed. I loved being around Jack, he was my emotional safety blanket, but at the same time, there seemed less and less room for him in my life now that I had my goal of losing weight. Secretly, I was pleased he had noticed. I was wearing my three-quarter-length jeans, a look I'd borrowed from Madonna. I was crazy about music and loved Madonna, U2, The Specials, Madness, The Beat and The Jam. Their posters adorned my room at home and every Sunday, I'd record The Charts on my cassette tape to listen to during the week.

'What?' I scoffed. 'Don't be stupid! It's the jeans, they're rubbish,' I replied casually.

'No, seriously,' he said, wide-eyed, tugging at my waistband to demonstrate his point. There was now a hand span between the material and my skin. 'You're getting really thin.'

That night, I ran home over the bridge at super speed – my plan was working really well! Unfortunately, it just wasn't fast enough for me and after a few weeks my weight seemed to plateau. Every day I weighed myself I was the same: just under eight stone. It was maddening, but I wasn't going to give up – it *had* to come off. In the shop near us, I scoured the magazines for tips on losing weight and in one I found the answer to my problems.

'The Cambridge Diet is a revolutionary new plan that allows you to lose weight FAST!' screamed the advert, next to a *before* and *after* picture of a woman. She was grotesque in the first picture – great big tree trunks for thighs, rolls of flab around her belly, and triple chins – but looked slim, fit and healthy in the next picture. This was the answer I'd been looking for. The plan consisted of drinking special nutritionally balanced shakes three times a day instead of eating. It was fast, effective and safe. What could be better? Unfortunately, at sixteen, I was too young to start the programme myself so I persuaded my Aunt Annette, my dad's twin sister, to arrange for a representative to visit us at her house – I didn't want my mum knowing.

'But Tina, love, you don't need to lose weight!' she objected at first. My aunt was lovely – whenever she came round, she always seemed to be on a diet, so I knew she'd be the right person to help me in my quest. If anyone would understand, it would be her.

'I just want to do it for a short while,' I replied innocently. 'It's all healthy so there's no problem. We'll do it together. Come on, it'll be fun!'

Eventually, she caved in and signed up to the plan and the representative left some boxes of the shake sachets for us. I took most of them, knowing Aunt Annette wouldn't have the stamina to last very long on the plan. And I was right: she gave in almost immediately, complaining they didn't taste of anything and she missed food too much. But for me – well, I found it easy. I hid the sachets in my room and made myself up one for breakfast, one for lunch and ate a normal meal for dinner. It was fine, I told myself. It was perfectly healthy because the shakes were nutritionally balanced. I was thrilled after the first week when I noticed the weight coming off really quickly.

One day in town, I went into Boots and noticed they had a digital-scales machine that gave you a whole printout of your weight and ideal weight. My God, it was like the Holy Grail of scales! So that became my new goal: to get there every day.

Now I was down to 7 stone 7 lb and, to help things along, I started to run 6 miles every day. Each afternoon, I'd go into town with 10p for my daily weigh-in at Boots, and seeing the pounds fall off gave me the most amazing buzz. I kept all the printed tickets like they were prizes, stored in my bedside drawer in neat little piles. Each day after my weigh-in, I was more and more motivated to lose the weight. And for the first time in years, I felt what I can only describe as happiness: this is what my life had been missing all this time – a goal, something I could aim for. And now I had one that made me feel so good about myself.

But as my quest took over, it began to push out other things in my life. Food, weight and calories became my world. Obsessed, I hoovered up books and magazines so that I could increase my knowledge of food. I could tell you, to the exact gram, every calorie, protein, fat, sugar and fibre of almost every type of food – I had it all memorised. My mind became a secret calculator, always counting up what everyone would be having and obviously what I would *not* be having.

My 'dinners', such as they were, had now become incredibly restrictive. I didn't eat meat anyway as I was a vegetarian, but now I cut out anything I thought would be fattening. Mostly, my meals were now a couple of pieces of Ryvita with a gossamer-thin layer of cream cheese, an apple and a little bit of carrot, cucumber or celery.

To friends and family, I became an accomplished liar in order to hide the extent of my diet. I told them: 'I'm just getting more into eating raw vegetables and fruit' or 'I'm full – I've just eaten' and, the favourite standby when all else failed: 'I don't like it.' Always there was a ready excuse in my mental arsenal to stop the questions and head off suspicion. But making food now took up a good part of my day. One morning I made a sandwich for my sister Katie with her favourite filling – bacon. I was so happy as I cut off the crusts very neatly and then laid down each slice of crispy bacon with forensic precision. But when I took it through to her, brimming with pride, I found she was still asleep in bed, dead to the world.

'Wake up, Katie!' I cooed softly into her ear, 'a lovely bacon sandwich for you here, just as you like it with tomato sauce and tons of butter. Come on, sleepyhead, wakey-wakey!'

Then I placed it next to her bed and left the room, thinking the smell would rouse her soon enough. But when I came back in later on that day, I found the empty plate next to the bin. Confused, I lifted the bin lid and was disgusted to see the whole sandwich, untouched, thrown away. I went berserk!

I stormed through to the lounge, shaking with rage: 'You didn't eat it, you cow! I made it for you especially and it was so tasty and good. How *could* you be so thoughtless and stupid?'

'Calm down,' Katie said, looking confused. 'It's just a sandwich, for God's sake! By the time I woke up it had gone cold so I didn't fancy it. What are you getting all worked up for?'

It was true – it *was* only a sandwich and I knew my reaction was completely over the top and disproportionate – but I couldn't help it. I needed to be around food, to see it, smell it, make it and yet deny myself even the tiniest morsel. If I ate any of it, I was weak and a complete failure. I had to maintain control at all times so that I could snatch my happiness through resisting the temptation. It took an iron will but I thrilled in testing myself over and over again.

I would sit for days, reading books about fats, trans fats, carbohydrates and the effects on the body. It consumed my every thought. If people were speaking to me, I would be watching their lips move but all the while I'd be thinking about calories or food intakes, or what exercise I could do next. These thoughts had replaced all other brain activity and I could not force them out of my head. There were times I did try to think of other things, but it was futile – it was an addiction and there was nothing I could do to stop it taking hold and it burning into my soul.

I read piles of newspapers, looking for recipes. It became an obsession to make hearty, fattening meals for my sisters and, of course, the challenge was never to eat a morsel myself. I baked bread, cakes and biscuits and insisted everyone have some, even if they weren't hungry. It gave me such a buzz to watch them munching down the food I'd made them. Even the toast I made them in the mornings was loaded with butter, right up to the edges!

It only took a few months for me to realise this wasn't normal. I had a new life in my head, a secret world nobody else had access to, and every day it seemed to get worse. I didn't feel the same any more and I didn't know why. I stopped going out to meet up with Diane and all of our friends, and even Jack, the love of my life, was fading into insignificance in my mind. There just wasn't room for him and I had no libido anyway – I didn't care about kissing him any more. I just wanted to get home and get stuck into my exercises. My sisters would see me every morning and night – jogging on the spot, crunching, squatting and jumping for hours – but they were used to their mad older sister with her latest crazes.

But I wanted to know what was happening. So, one day, when I was in the library, taking notes from recipe books to get ideas about what to cook for my sisters, I wandered over to the Personal Development Section. There, I found a book on eating disorders. I borrowed it and ran home straight away to read it. Lying on my bed that day, I devoured the book with hungry fascination. There was a name for what I'd become: anorexic. It talked about all the ways in which food and weight loss became an obsession for its sufferers. There was an example of a girl – Cathy, not her real name – she'd lost 3 stone and was so thin, you could see her ribcage through her skin.

It's funny, but it didn't disturb me at all to read about anorexia; if anything, it was a little comforting. I'd never heard of eating disorders before now and I was happy to think that there were others like me out there. It was nice to know there was a name for my condition and there was no mention of potentially fatal consequences. It just said that sufferers became very thin, cold and their hair and teeth suffered.

Looking at the picture of Cathy, I was suddenly filled with new resolve. Three stone? I could lose more than that! It was like the gauntlet had been thrown down and now I had a new goal: I was going to be the best, most complex anorexic in the world! I would benchmark the illness to a whole new level.

I was thrilled to reach the milestone of seven stone by November 1985. It had seemed so far away when I was 9 stone, but now I was there, it proved just how easy it was. And I resolved to keep going. Of course I didn't realise that in the grip of anorexia, my brain was now being starved of nutrients to perform properly and make rational decisions. In my mind there was nothing more sensible than continuing my quest for the perfect body and 7 stone was just way too big for me. I had to keep going – I had no idea what my target weight actually was but I thought I'd know when I got there. The more weight I lost, the more I piled on the layers of clothing to hide my skinny frame and the less I saw of my friends.

One day, on a visit to see us, Dad made a passing comment.

'Tina, you've lost a lot of weight.'

It was a throwaway remark, no judgement or tone that made me think he felt either good or bad about this and, outwardly at least, I ignored this observation and talked about other things. But inside, I was dancing with delight. What a boost! In fact, it gave me such a high that I rewarded myself by going to my room to exercise for the next three hours. *You've got to make sure that the next time he sees you, you are even thinner!* said the voice in my head.

Now my routine was strictly and entirely based on food and exercise. I was up at 5 a.m. to start my exercises and then, two hours later, I'd get the family up with breakfast, cornflakes and toast, and watch them eat it. I walked Celine to her school, two miles away, and then ran all the way home at a sprint. During the day, I would go to the library to study recipe books, hang around the Wellgate or head to the swimming pool, where I'd clock up hundreds of laps at a time, followed by some light weight training.

In the afternoon, I visited Boots for my daily weigh-in and my whole mood depended on whether I'd lost another pound. If I had, I'd be happy for the rest of the day; if I was still the same as the day before, a black mood would descend and I'd have to push myself even harder in my night-time exercises to ensure that the next day I got a pound off.

My schooling was non-existent now as it was getting in the way of my obsession. I had all but given up and my mum never said anything.

It wasn't until I reached 6 stone 10 pounds that someone noticed the dramatic change, and not in a good way. I was walking through the Wellgate shopping centre with my friend Paula and all of a sudden she turned and looked at me; her eyes widened in horror. She pointed down to my sternum – that day, I was wearing a crew-necked, black sweater – and I wondered what she was looking at.

'Oh, my God, Tina!' she whispered as her eyes filled with tears.

'What?' I snapped, annoyed at her dramatics. 'What is it?'

'Tina, look at your bones!' she breathed. The look on her face was horrible – fear, pity, sadness and disgust all rolled into one.

'Oh, Tina! Oh, my goodness, you're too skinny,' she burbled. 'You've lost too much weight.'

She was really quite upset but I thought she was being completely over the top – I knew for a FACT that I had not lost enough weight so she was just being silly. Of course, secretly, in the back of my mind, I was pleased that someone had noticed my efforts.

But it couldn't last. One day, when I was running low on shakes, I called my auntie to ask her to reorder.

'I'm sorry, Tina,' she sighed over the phone. 'It's just too expensive. I can't afford to buy them for you any more.'

This was a disaster. I felt completely thrown – how was I to cope if I couldn't get the shakes any more? That night, I made a huge pot of broth. It was meant to feed the entire family but because I felt so scared and uncertain, I lost it: I ate the whole pot in one sitting.

Urgh! I felt sick, not just from the large quantity of food, which by now I was no longer used to, but because I had failed; I had lost my willpower. My mind turned on me. *You are so pathetic and weak, Tina!* it shrieked. *You're just a lazy, horrible worthless slob!* The words rang out in my ears – it was deafening. I couldn't tell any more if this was the voice or me – it just felt like my head was going to explode. In a blind panic, I rushed to the toilet and spent the next hour getting rid of it all, and trying to erase the guilt at the same time.

As I gasped and retched over the toilet bowl, I tasted the metallic flavour of blood. My fingers were bleeding where my back molars had cut into them. After an hour, my throat, lips and neck were all swollen and my eyes bloodshot and streaming. The swelling affected my hearing and for a while, it felt like I was deaf. My stomach ached with the forced convulsions. I couldn't even speak properly as the vomiting had damaged my throat. It was a nightmare but at least I had purged all the food.

Lying on my bed that night, my head spinning, I realised I was no good at making myself sick. I hated it – the whole process of eating, drinking lots of water and then spending lots of time trying to be sick without making horrible noises. It was repulsive and I knew I couldn't keep it up but without the shakes, I would be unable to control my food intake properly. There was only one thing for it: I had to stop eating altogether. It was the only way to maintain complete control.

So that's what I did.

My new super-duper diet would now consist of: Diet Coke or Diet Pepsi, no-sugar squash, black coffee and any cigarettes I could pinch from my mum. That's it. For months, I continued with my quest and my weight dropped even faster. It was a revelation and a great one, I thought.

Chapter 7

At War With My Body

Huddling under a thin blanket, I pulled my legs up to my chest and hooked my arms under my knees to try to contain the little warmth I felt. It was freezing! FREEZING! Next to me, my sisters slept soundly, all in their thin nighties as if it was the height of summer. But it wasn't summer! It was now near the end of November and it seemed no matter how many layers I wore, I was always chilled to the bone. Right now, I was wearing three layers of leggings, two T-shirts and a sweater and still my fingers felt numb with cold. It didn't help that we didn't have central heating and no money to feed the electric heater, but how come the others slept so well?

The layers now stayed on all the time. I told myself it was to stave off the freezing winters but inside I knew there was another reason: I didn't want anybody to see how thin I'd become. Anorexia, this was my secret, and I didn't want anybody to take it away. The fact was the more I starved myself, the happier I seemed to feel. Some days I felt completely euphoric at my discipline and control.

The only time I allowed my body to be seen was when I went swimming. In the past couple of weeks, I'd set myself a new task. Every day I ran down to Olympia, our local pool, and pushed myself to do 100 laps a day.

I was three weeks into my starvation diet when my body started to rebel. I'd just swum hard for an hour and was on my way back to the changing room when suddenly I was overcome with nausea. Thinking I was about to throw up, I ran into the toilet cubicle and fainted.

I came to lying on the toilet floor, just as the cleaner was trying to drag me out by my arms. She'd spotted my hands poking out from under the door, she explained, as she pulled me upright and sat me on a chair. Then, as I tried to stabilise the wobbly feeling that had infected my whole body, she instructed me to lean forward, placing my head between my legs. It was a shock that this had happened to me and I tried to stave off her matronly fussing by insisting I was fine. But my overall feeling was one of annoyance: it irritated me that I'd been caught out like this and I resolved not to let it happen again. To prove the point, I stood up, got dressed and walked the three miles home.

From then on, I made sure I controlled the fainting. As soon as I got that strange woozy feeling, I'd nibble on a Ryvita cracker or eat a tiny piece of apple. That way I could give my body a small energy boost that would make me feel normal again. It worked a treat and every time I succeeded in heading off a fainting fit I gave myself a mental pat on the back. I was so clever, so smart!

I knew my plan was working brilliantly because I could now try on every single item of clothing in BHS and they were all too big for me, massive even. It gave me such a thrill to realise that I could fit into every single piece of clothing in that store. Though I didn't have any money to buy clothes, I started browsing the children's sections. What age could I fit? I almost giggled to myself as I realised that I was so small, I could probably squeeze into a children's pair of jeans, aged ten.

Meanwhile, my old life was falling away from me, bit by bit, and that was a good thing – I had no time now for distractions like school or boyfriends. I hadn't seen Jack in nearly two weeks when he called me on the phone one night. I'd been doing my exercises in my bedroom when my sister Katy called out to me from the corridor. I braced myself. I'd been expecting this and I was ready when he asked in a hesitant, nervous voice if I was okay.

'Yeah, I'm fine,' I said matter-of-factly. 'However, I've got some issues I need to deal with right now and I'm really sorry but I can't see you any more.'

I knew I should have been sad but actually I was relieved at the chance to get rid of Jack. It just wasn't possible to juggle the demands of a boyfriend when I needed all my energy to focus on my quest.

There was something resigned in his voice when he replied: 'Yeah. Okay – I mean, I'm really sorry about that, Tina, but I understand. And, well, I'm here for you whenever you need me.'

He didn't seem surprised at all – he must have known I'd been avoiding him and expected me to end things when he called. That was why he sounded so nervous and awkward. For my part, I just wanted him off the phone as quickly as possible. There was nothing more to be said so I thanked him quickly and ended things with a casual 'Bye' before putting down the receiver. Phew! Now I could concentrate 100 per cent on what I was doing, no more people in the way.

The more time passed, the more my body began to fight back. The cold and the fainting fits were bad enough but now I started to suffer with terrible pains in my stomach. They never seemed to leave and though I tried hard to ignore them, they just got worse and worse. One afternoon, they were so bad I couldn't ignore them any longer. Doubled over in pain, I called out to my mum.

'I think I need to see a doctor,' I gasped, gripping my stomach. It was excruciating! Mum nodded sympathetically and ordered me to bed, saying she would call him straight away.

It didn't take long. Within the hour, Mum's favourite doctor was stood at my bedroom door. Dr Coburn was tall, with bushy brown hair and a large moustache. He must have been in his fifties and Mum thought he was quite handsome. She hung back in the doorway as he came in and sat down on my bed. I didn't waste any time – relieved to see a professional, I helpfully pulled down the blanket and pulled up my nightie to show him my stomach, the cause of my agony.

But Dr Coburn seemed to have other ideas. Almost

immediately, he pulled my nightie down again and replaced the cover on top of me. With a serious look on his face he told me straight: 'Tina, I don't need to see your tummy. You are anorexic and you need help.'

His manner was so abrupt, so brusque that I was shocked. I looked over at my mum, but she didn't seem to flinch. She knew what he was going to say. So she'd noticed! All this time, I thought I'd been so clever at hiding my illness and yet she knew all along. All of a sudden, the penny dropped and I realised they had been planning this all along. This wasn't what I expected at all – this was an ambush, a siege. I burst into tears.

A little softer now, Dr Coburn explained: 'Your mother called me some months back – she was very concerned about you and wanted my advice. I had to tell her that because you are now sixteen, I can't help you until you ask me for help. Now you've called for me and I want to help you. Tina, this has been a long time coming and, right now, you need urgent medical treatment as you are very, very ill. Dangerously ill.'

It was so unfair, and so wrong! He didn't even seem interested in my stomach pain. What kind of a doctor was he, anyway? Wiping away my angry tears with the heel of my hand, I clamped my lips together and silently seethed. When he'd finished his little pre-rehearsed speech, I told him vehemently: 'I'm fine, Dr Coburn. Don't be so stupid! I'm not ill – I've just got a sore tummy! It will pass.'

Meanwhile, Mum sucked in her breath, crossed her arms and drew up her shoulders, as if trying to hug herself. I could see now the anxiety in her eyes and the pain on her face.

All this time she'd been concerned about me and yet she'd never said a word! Now she bit her bottom lip as Dr Coburn went on again, telling me things I didn't want to hear. I tuned him out – it was words, just words. He couldn't make me do anything; none of them could. I couldn't believe I'd been so stupid to call for help. Inside, I reproached myself for letting my guard down.

Eventually, after about fifteen minutes, Dr Coburn gave up. He sighed and stood up and then turned to face my mum, who looked crestfallen.

'I'm sorry.' He shook his head. 'I tried, I can't force her.' Then he left and Mum shut the door behind him. I heard muffled voices from the corridor and the unmistakable sound of my mum sobbing. Then, after I heard the front door close, she came back into my room. Her eyes were red and her voice broke as she said: 'Tina, you really, really need help! I've been trying to get you help for months. Please listen to the doctor.'

'There's nothing to worry about,' I spat back angrily. 'I have it under control. Trust me – now just leave me alone!'

After she left, I lay there, fists balled in anger at my sides. How could I have been so careless? It never occurred to me that Mum would see what was going on. I had to be even more careful from now on. They didn't understand. There was no reason for their concern – none of them understood that I was on top of this thing. I was in control; I just had to get a little thinner and then everything would be okay. I knew I could go further and I had to push on, no matter what!

After this close call, I was determined more than ever to prove I was fine by losing weight and staying healthy, but every day that passed brought a fresh round of misery for my failing body. My periods had stopped for a couple of months, my hair started to fall out and my skin started to flake off. Peeling off the last layer of clothing always brought with it a layer of skin. It was so dry – no matter how much moisturiser I rubbed on myself, translucent flecks of skin peppered my clothing. It was disgusting – and to make matters worse, I'd grown this really long hair over my body, repulsing me even further. Still, I ignored these failings as much as I could – I only had one thing on my mind: getting thinner.

Now I started to use laxatives since my energy levels were really low and it was getting harder and harder to complete my exercise regime. Yet I had to push myself further or I would never achieve my dream. The drugs played havoc with my bowel movements. I was determined to flush out every little thing inside me – in fact, nothing much came out of me these days except a weird, green slime, like mucus. I couldn't tell anybody. Of course not! I could never admit to any weakness whatsoever – that had nearly tripped me up the last time. Instead, I retreated further and further into myself, cloaking my illness with deception and lies.

In early December, Sophie, now aged twelve, asked me if I would walk with her into town to buy some books. Pleased at the chance of a little exercise, I agreed, though just before we left, I ate a whole box of Ex-Lax squares. Usually, I was able to time my body's reaction to this, but today was very different. We walked for about fifteen minutes and suddenly my whole body started to burn and ache. I thought I was going to pass out with the searing pain that was ripping through me.

In desperation, I took flight, running to the local public toilet. Inside, the revolting stench of urine filled my nostrils but I didn't care. Already, I could feel the fluid running down my legs. *Oh, fuck! Oh, fuck!* I couldn't control it – it was just coming out!

I slammed the door behind me and fell onto the stinking toilet floor, vomiting all over the place. The fluid from my bowel was now uncontrollably flooding out of my back passage and going everywhere. I could feel it seeping through the three pairs of leggings I was wearing under my jeans. It was not even faeces, more like dark, watery slime. It was so painful.

OH, CHRIST! My heart pounded and I started to shake and cry at the same time. *I'm dying! I'm dying!* I could literally feel my intestines twisting inside me. Now my tears mixed with the vomit and I felt my hair sticking to my face. I was incapable of moving off the floor where I'd collapsed, hanging off the toilet bowl as if clinging to the wreckage of a sinking ship.

Eventually, I heard footsteps and then a tentative knock at the door.

'Are you okay, Tina?' came Sophie's scared little voice. Poor thing – she sounded terrified. She must have heard it all! And yet I still couldn't let my guard down, couldn't let her see what a mess I'd become. So I lied. I lied from behind the door, where I was covered in all sorts of shit and vomit. In my worst pretend-happy voice, I sang out: 'Yes, I'm okay, Sophie. I'll be out in a minute.'

Inside, I wanted to scream and cry for help. I wanted her

to run home and fetch Mum. But my resolute attitude of never letting anyone see my weakness overrode everything: I HAD to stay in control, no matter what! So I waited until I no longer felt sick and tried to clean myself up with the cheap shiny pieces of toilet paper I found lying around. I tried to use two small squares of paper to clean my face, very unsuccessfully, and eventually exited the toilet, avoiding my sister's eyes.

'Sorry, Sophie,' I muttered, my voice full of shame. 'I've got to go home and change, 'cos I've had an accident and need a shower.'

Sophie didn't reply and we walked home in silence. I was so grateful that I was wearing so many layers of clothing or she might have seen the horrible mess under my jeans. But she must have smelled it and she didn't say a word to me the whole way home. I decided during that terrible walk never to use laxatives again. It had caught me off-guard and I couldn't allow that.

Once safely at home, I scrubbed myself clean and washed my clothes in the sink. Then I steeled myself to looked at my reflection in the mirror. And I hated what I saw: I felt a mixture of anger for still being fat and revulsion at the state of me. There was no difference any more between the voice and me – it had filled up my head completely.

I was ugly beyond belief. I was a horrible, fat, weak, insignificant person who was taking up far too much space in the world and needed to disappear to allow others to be happy. Look how I'd upset my sister! She didn't need that kind of trauma in her life. I couldn't bear the thought of hurting her, my mum or my other sisters – the people I loved most in the world – any longer.

No, it would just be better for everyone if I died. I knew now that I was in a terrible place and beyond help. Suddenly, calmness flooded my brain. This was my epiphany, the moment everything became clear. I knew now what my goal was – I wanted to starve myself to death. Being thinner wasn't good enough – I must die, and the quicker the better.

So I continued on my path with new resolve and, two weeks later, I collapsed in my bedroom. I came to on the floor but, instead of picking myself up, as I usually did after a fainting fit, I found I couldn't move. Frightened, I called out for my mum, who responded with lightening speed.

'Tina!' she gasped as I lay on my back. I tried to focus but it felt like I was floating away, like wisps of smoke in the air.

'I can't get up,' I said. 'I can't move.'

I was so ill, so weak now that even these few words took a tremendous effort of will and concentration. I was dying, I knew that. Mum picked me up gently and lay me on my bed. I felt myself fading in and out a little, not really aware of the passing of time. Moments later, it seemed to me, Dr Coburn was at my side but his voice came from far away.

'Tina, I've arranged for you to go into the hospital now and your mum will get your stuff.'

But I didn't care. I didn't care about anything any more – I sensed myself slipping down a long tunnel, further and further away from reality. Out of nowhere, my dad appeared and, together, him and Mum half-carried, half-walked me to the ambulance waiting outside our flat. The drive to the hospital felt very long but, once there, I was eased into a wheelchair and pushed along the stark white corridors. As the neon light-strips flashed above me, I noted my parents' concerned faces. *Oh, well,* I thought dreamily to myself, *not long to go – it will all be over soon.*

Chapter 8

Are There Calories in Air?

As soon as I was wheeled into the ward, a tall lady, who introduced herself as Sister Cummings, showed me into her little office. Panic now rose within me. I felt a surge of energy as the accompanying adrenalin kicked in.

Sister Cummings had short and curly fair hair and her large eyes and generous, full lips reminded me of Princess Anne. She seemed at pains to reassure me that I was in the right place.

'Tina, we're so pleased you're here,' she said, smiling, her warm eyes crinkling at the corners. 'We've had many girls here over the years, perhaps not as young as you, but all with the same condition. And we can help you – you just have to let us help you.'

Unable to focus fully on her words, I took in only the basics of what she was telling me. There would be a strict eating programme, a system that rewarded weight gain and positively reinforced the importance of getting well. After putting on 2 lb, I would gain access to a radio, another 2lb would buy me some time with a newspaper, another 2 lb, a phone call, and so on . . .

My attention snapped back when she said: '. . . the important thing is that you are never left alone at any time. Even going to the toilet, you will be accompanied by a nurse. Your privacy privileges will begin when you have proved that you are committed to gaining weight.'

Suddenly, my head started to pound and my anxiety levels shot up. They were going to try to make me fat by denying me my dignity! How could I possibly go to the toilet in front of a total stranger? I couldn't cope with anyone seeing me naked. Seemingly oblivious to my rising panic, Sister Cummings went on: 'The meals are made up of very high-fat foods and no fibre, since we understand that laxative abuse has been a feature of your illness . . .'

NO WAY! My brain screamed out. NO WAY ARE YOU PEOPLE GOING TO MAKE ME FAT!

Eventually, she came to the clincher: '. . . and to begin with, we will have you on bed rest, with no getting up or going out for a cigarette until you put on 8 pounds.'

'*What?* I can't even smoke?' I finally exploded. From somewhere deep inside, I felt a rush of energy and stood bolt upright.

'That's it,' I snapped. 'I'm not staying! I'm out of here, I'm not ready for this.'

And before anybody could stop me, I walked out. I strode down the corridor, the corridor that I'd just been wheeled down minutes before, as fast as I possibly could, ignoring the plaintive shouts from my parents behind me. I could see I needed to get up to the next level in order to exit the hospital but, just looking at the stairs, I knew the little strength I had would never carry me up, so I punched the button on the lift and got in. It seemed crazy that I had been so weak just moments earlier, almost willing death to come, and yet now I was walking around. All I knew was that I had to get out of there as quickly as possible.

Catching me up, my parents got in the lift behind me. For the first time in years, they were as one: their looks of utter disgust matched each other's perfectly. They were fuming with me, speechless with rage. After literally throwing me into the back of the car, we started for the journey home – I smoked all the way back. I could feel their resentment and hostility from the back seat but I switched off from it and concentrated instead on the houses whizzing by outside and on smoking as many cigarettes as possible.

When we arrived back home, Mum got out of the car without a word and Dad just drove off. I ran up the stairs to our tiny flat and slammed my bedroom door shut on them all. After curling up on my bed, I pretended to fall asleep. I was so angry that I had nearly been tricked into eating and getting help. It was the closest call I'd had so far. From inside me came a strange, happy feeling from my determination and my win: I would never give this illness up, I promised myself. *Never!*

I went on avoiding foods for another few weeks and once again tried to ignore the cold, the pain and the fact that my skin had turned a horrible bluey-grey colour. I tried to ignore the brittle, broken hair that came off on my pillow every night.

Coldness was now a permanent state for me – I hated taking off my clothes for any reason, even to change into my pyjamas. My gums bled all the time and my bowels were just a seething mass of pain. There was nothing coming out of me except green yellowish mucus, like jelly. It was awful when the slime oozed out as it made me feel sick and yet at the same time I felt like I had achieved something by emptying my whole body of food. The tiny amounts of urine I managed to squeeze out were deep red, like beetroot juice.

But it still wasn't enough; I wasn't thin enough. I'd test myself by pinching the parchment-thin skin on my arms or legs, convinced the thin slither beneath my fingers was fat – horrible, wretched fat. My one comfort was to measure my weight loss by holding my hands around my upper thighs and waist and squish in. The fingers would touch and, as the gap widened between my body and my hands, so too did my happy smile. I pushed and pushed each day until the weight fell off me. Each day I ran to Boots for my weigh-in – I was 6 stone now but stopping was no longer an option.

Two weeks later, I ran to the post office to buy a stamp to send a letter to my Irish pen pal, who like me was also a huge U2 fan. Every few months, we'd write to one another, just silly stuff about the band, nothing real about our lives. But as I went to lick the stamp, I froze. The back of the stamp! My mind suddenly whirred – *it's sweet! It must have sugar in it. Calories! Oh, no! No, no, no! I can't lick this stamp, I'll get fat!* Instead, I licked my finger and rubbed that on the back of the stamp. But as I posted the letter through the box, panic bubbled up within me. *There must be hidden calories in everything – everywhere! I can't escape them! I'll always be fat because I'm probably consuming calories through the air without even realising it.*

I walked home in a daze – now my head felt very strange and I was consumed with despair. *I'm inhaling calories right now, right this very minute!* my brain screamed out in anguish. *How can I control the calories I can't see?* I knew there was only one way – I had to try to take very small breaths. Now my rational sense had all but deserted me as I resolved to limit the air I breathed in. Of course, I couldn't stop breathing altogether but I had to try to make a difference. These tormenting thoughts chased themselves around my head, day and night now – I barely slept with the worry that by falling asleep I'd lose control of my breathing.

I was still trying to exercise but now, weak and exhausted, I could barely manage 50 sit-ups at a time. Added to that, I was trying to stop myself panting while I did them. The pressure inside my head was unbearable, immense, and I was so tortured by my racing thoughts that I felt like I was losing a grip on reality.

When I saw anybody eating now, I was filled with loathing for their lack of control, their greed! Just watching my mum eat her toast in the mornings was agonising – I wanted to shake her and tell her to stop. How could she be so weak? Anyone who ate was a weak-minded worthless piece of shit, I was convinced. I couldn't have willed anything past my lips now even if I had wanted to eat; it simply wasn't possible.

One morning, three weeks after my failed hospital admission, I woke up and went to take a shower. I don't know why but for some reason I'd forgotten to lock the door. Just as I was finishing up, my sister Katie came in to use the toilet. I was in my towel and had pulled up my knickers when it occurred to me to have some fun. On TV there was an advert for Scotch videotapes. It was such a catchy little song and I knew I now looked so thin it would be an accurate impression of the cartoon skeleton in the ad. I thought she would find it hilarious. So I dropped the towel and started to sing: 'I'm going to tell you how it's going to be with Scotch's lifetime guarantee . . .'

I jumped around in my pants, my stick-thin legs and arms jutting out at every angle.

'Record what you want, both night and day. Then rerecord, don't fade away . . .'

I thought she'd fall about laughing but, instead, Katie's eyes widened in horror and she burst into tears, fleeing the bathroom with her face in her hands. I stopped and stood still. In that terrible moment, I had seen what my sister saw – I had seen her look of horror, disgust and . . . and . . . oh, God, hatred! *Yes*, hatred! She hated me right then. The way she'd looked at me – so scared – as if I was a monster. I looked down at the blue skin stretched taut over my bones and the cold hard realisation hit me: it was enough.

It looked as if my skin was shrink-wrapped over my whole body. In the mirror, my huge teeth dominated my skull-like face and my skin was grey and lifeless. My eyes were dead.

It was time. The look in my sister's eyes had told me everything I needed to know: I was an ugly monster and I needed help. Silently, and with a heavy heart, I got dressed and went to find my mum.

'I want to go to the hospital,' I told her, my voice cracking with sadness. What a pathetic thing I had become. Shame engulfed me. 'I want to get help.'

Mum rewarded me with a huge smile and told me how pleased she was to finally hear that. She had the number for Sister Cummings by the phone and called it straight away. I heard the tiny voice down the line from where I stood, just a foot away. 'Bring her in as soon as you can,' Sister Cummings instructed. 'We've been waiting for your call – the bed has been ready the whole time.'

Later, as I packed my toothbrush, nightie, fluffy peach dressing gown and slippers into a hold-all in my bedroom, I asked Mum: 'Why did they keep the bed for me?'

'They knew, honey. They knew it would be only a matter of weeks,' she replied sorrowfully. *A matter of weeks until what?* I wondered. And then it dawned on me: until I either asked for help or died. I was struck with misery then. I hadn't realised what everyone else had known for a while – Mum, Dad, my sisters, the professionals . . . I'd no idea it was that serious. The ambulance arrived and, in a matter of hours, I was back at the hospital again. The one I had left so hurriedly, three weeks earlier.

And instantly, I regretted it.

Chapter 9

Humiliation

My one crumb of comfort about finally admitting I needed to go to hospital was the thought that at least there, I would be warm. It was December, almost Christmas, in fact, and I was so tired of shivering and piling on layers of clothes just to stave off the feeling that I was going to die of cold. On top of that, I knew I would be in hospital over the holidays, which was a relief. Since my parents had split up, our Christmases were now sad, tense affairs. Usually, Dad came over for lunch but the effort of trying to be civil to each other was always too much for my parents and it would inevitably end in conflict and tears. At least here, in hospital, I would be protected from the ugliness of it all.

I needed a break — I knew that. Still, I couldn't quite get my head around being in a hospital. Hospitals were for sick people and I didn't feel sick, just tired. Exhausted actually, mentally and physically.

As soon as we arrived, my parents were asked to leave. I was now in the care of the ward, they explained, but I'd be able to see them again when I was a little better. Then I was shown to the bed that was to be my home for the next few months – bed one in bay one, right in front of the nurses' station – and asked to change into my pyjamas. They pulled the curtain round the bed but a nurse in a starched white uniform and white nurse's hat stayed on my side of it.

As I tried to peel off my clothes, layer upon painful layer, the short, dark Filipino nurse with the thick glasses and shiny black hair introduced herself as Fiona.

'Can't you leave while I get undressed?' I asked, a little testily.

'I'm sorry, dear,' she said, shaking her head, and I noted her accent was an exotic mix of Scottish and Asian. 'You're just going to have to get used to having me around, I'm afraid. This is what it's going to be like from now on – one of us will always be here.'

I was stunned – what? No privacy at all? It felt so degrading but I really didn't have any choice. Gently, I lifted my arms and started to pull off my shirt. As I got down to the final T-shirt and leggings, I saw my skin falling away in big flakes to expose red, sore patches underneath. Too weak to stand any more, I collapsed on the ground. I didn't care if she saw me now – I was beyond caring. Fiona helped me onto the bed and, slowly and gently, helped me put my pyjamas on. Then she went out, before returning, a minute later, with a wheelchair.

'We've got to get you to the bathroom, love, to the weigh chair.'

I let her ease me into the chair and wheel me to the large

white bathroom at the end of the corridor, where there was a chair attached to an old-fashioned set of metal scales with the sliders along the side. Once I was safely on, Fiona measured – I was 6 stone exactly. The number filled me with excitement and pride. Then she wheeled me back to bed.

After a little while, Sister Cummings came in to see me, sitting down at the end of my bed. They had already worked out my specific goals and she handed me a sheet of paper outlining my programme for recovery. I read the list of goals and accompanying privileges with horror.

At 6 stone 2 lb, I could get an hour of radio; 6 stone 4 lb, an hour of newspapers; 6 stone 6 lb, an hour of writing materials; 6 stone 8 lb, a cigarette; 6 stone 10 lb, a phone call; 6 stone 12 lb, TV for an hour; and so on. I wouldn't even be allowed to go to the bathroom on my own until I reached 7 stone 7 lb, and I couldn't see any of my friends or family until 7 stone 8 lb.

The goal was to reach my 'ideal' weight, which was set at 8 stone 7 pounds. I nearly laughed when I read that. It was impossible for me to imagine gaining weight now – in my mind, this list was as unachievable as asking me to fly to the moon. Sister gave me some medication, which she said would help me sleep and perhaps give me a bit of an appetite, which again gave me a little kick: I knew nothing would make me feel hungry – only I could control that – but I took the tablets anyway and slept that night like a baby.

At 6.30 a.m. sharp the next morning, I was rudely awakened by the bustle and noise of the nurses rushing around. The blinds were pulled up sharply to allow the light to stream in and, for the first time, I got a good look at the people around me. It was a surprise to see the other beds weren't full of thin young girls like myself – instead, I was met by the sight of people of all different shapes and sizes. When Fiona came to check on me, I asked her what kind of ward I was on.

'Acute psychiatric, dear,' she replied. 'There are people here with all different types of mental illness, not just anorexia.'

At that moment, the lady in the bed next to me started to cry and Fiona walked over to deal with her. Mental illness? I had a mental illness? The thought had never even crossed my mind. In the far corner in a side room, I heard the sound of a baby crying, then I noticed a woman shuffling towards us in her slippers – she looked like she was still half asleep. Her eyelids drooped lazily over unseeing eyes and, suddenly, I felt very frightened. Fiona must have sensed my unease because after she'd dealt with the crying lady, she came back to me and started chatting about herself in a calm, friendly way. She told me she'd come over from the Philippines some years before and that she had two children of her own.

'Now come on, Tina,' she urged, 'it's time to get you to the weigh chair.'

'What, again?' I was confused.

'Yes, every morning – this is what we do.'

I was thrilled to find I was one pound lighter that morning – 5 stone 13 lb, my lowest weight to date! After the weigh in, I needed the toilet, so Fiona led me to one of the cubicles in the bathroom. She handed me a small pan to pee into since they had to monitor what was coming in and going out. I took the pan and walked into the loo, expecting her to stand outside the door, but she followed me right in and stood there.

'Please, can you please leave me now?' I begged, horrified.

'No, I can't, Tina,' she explained, in a kind but firm voice. 'This is the policy until you start to put the weight on. Don't worry, I've seen it all before. There's nothing to be embarrassed about.'

Still, I was mortified and so tense I knew there was no way I could do anything if she was standing there, looking straight at me.

'Well, can't you at least turn your back?' I pleaded. So that's what she did. Even so, I was so shy and embarrassed, I couldn't do anything.

I was accompanied back to bed and, about twenty minutes later, the food arrived. Oh, God, it was my worst nightmare come true! There were two slices of thick, white toast, scored to soak up what looked like a tonne of butter, a bowl of Rice Krispies and a vanilla milkshake.

'What's all this?' I was reeling. 'Why have you given me so much food? There's enough for four people here!'

'That's the "Build Up",' said Fiona. 'And you better get used to it because there will be at least seven of these every day.'

Gobsmacked, I just sat there, looking at the tray in horror. Another nurse arrived and gave me my medication. When I asked her what it was, she told it was just something to help me relax. I took the medicine without question but, after the nurse left, I turned to look at Fiona with despair, my eyes filled with hot, angry tears.

'Why the hell are you giving me so much food, Fiona?' It was so upsetting to see all this in front of me – I couldn't believe they imagined I could even begin to eat any of it. Butter was atrocious, just pure calories – I hadn't touched it in years. I'd always hated the greasy taste.

But Fiona fixed me with a serious look.

'Tina, you know you are very ill. You need to get better and the foods we give you will get the weight on so you can start to heal and get well.'

'But, Fiona, this is all fatty food and I don't eat fat! There are no vitamins or fibre in white toast and butter and I don't drink milk so I can't have all this stuff.'

'Tina, please don't worry about what you are eating and just try a tiny piece. We're going to take this one step at a time. The shakes are full of goodness so don't you worry.'

But I couldn't even countenance eating a single morsel of the food. Instead, I took a tiny sip of the drink – it tasted like vanilla ice cream and my head swam with the awful realisation that it must contain a million calories! Nope, I wasn't going to have any of it.

So I folded my arms resolutely, turned out my bottom lip and told her straight: 'I can't eat this, it's just pure fat.'

After an hour, Fiona finally gave up and, as she took the tray away, she told me, a little annoyed: 'Tina, you will never put weight on refusing food.'

But I felt victorious – I couldn't give away my control that easily.

Little did I know, this was just the first battle in a very long war. At 10 a.m., another Build Up arrived and more toast, which I also refused. Two hours later, lunch came.

'What the heck is *that*?' I asked, disgusted. It looked like two massive scoops of mashed potato under the thickest layer of yellow cheese I had ever seen. Since I could not remember the last time I'd eaten cheese, I refused that, too. As the food kept coming and I refused each meal, my excuses got more and more elaborate. They were providing me with a vegetarian diet but now I insisted I was a vegan, too.

'I don't eat cheese, eggs, gelatine, butter, chocolate, milk, pastry . . .' I reeled off a long list of items that to all intents and purposes excluded me from eating anything they put in front of me. Day after day it went on: the food arrived, I refused, and they took it away again, just to replace it with something equally hideous and unappealing, two hours later. The nurses did their best, trying to coax me to have a bite of each meal, but I was resolute. Funnily enough, as the days went on, the medication kicked in and, though I was still refusing food, my anxiety had now dropped significantly.

'Can't you just start me on something like an apple or Ryvita?' I suggested to Fiona. I thought I was being helpful. The whole idea that I would eat this fatty food just seemed so ridiculous; it felt like they were being stupid. *They must realise this isn't going to work*, I thought. *I can't go from no food whatsoever to wolfing down huge fatty meals seven times a day!*

The whole time, I wasn't allowed to leave my bed except to go to the weigh chair or the toilet. Every calorie counted, they explained, so I wasn't allowed to move until I started gaining weight. In frustration, I spent my time trying to clench any tiny bit of imaginary muscle I had left in my body in an attempt to burn calories. Whenever the nurse moved away from me, I flapped my arms up and down and bicycle-wheeled my legs under the covers. I would also make my whole body rigid for as long as possible. As soon as someone appeared at my side, I'd stop – I couldn't trust anybody in there, I knew that much.

After four days of refusing food, the dietician came to see me. She was a lovely lady in her early twenties – short with strawberry-blonde hair – but she didn't stand a chance.

'You're so malnourished, Tina, you have to eat foods that replenish the vitamins, protein and iron you are lacking,' she tried to explain. 'You might even have to consider eating meat or fish again to get the proteins back in you.'

At this, I actually laughed in her face. AS IF! The more she talked, the less I listened. Frankly, I was more of an expert on food, nutrients and diet than anybody, I was sure of that.

Finally, exasperated, she said: 'Look, you tell us what you would like to eat and we'll make it for you especially.'

'I'm a vegetarian,' I explained as if to a child, 'so I only eat vegetables.'

'Oh-kay,' she responded. 'Well, why don't we make you steamed vegetables in a cheese sauce?'

'NO!' I erupted. 'I'm not going to eat cheese, I told you that already!'

And so she left, rather cross at me, and my weight continued to drop. The only thing I allowed to pass my lips was water and medication. They thought they could break me down and that, eventually, I'd snap, but I had such an iron will, I knew they could never force me to give up control. In fact, in the end, it wasn't force that they used.

After a week, a new nurse arrived at my bedside with the morning Build Up. She was short – only about 5 feet tall – comfortably round and had grey hair and a nervous manner. I reckoned her to be about sixty years old. As usual, I took one look at the tray and told her I wasn't going to touch it.

The little old lady, who reminded me of my granny, seemed mortified. Her eyes widened as she leaned in to me and whispered: 'I'm going to get into trouble, dearie, if you don't eat any of it.'

For a moment, I wavered – I didn't want to get this sweet old lady into trouble with her superiors. But what if it was a trick? Could I trust her?

'Really? Are you *really* going to get into trouble?' I whispered back, looking about me furtively, in case any of the other nurses were nearby. They were so mean, it didn't surprise me that they took out their frustrations on the lower-ranking nurses.

She nodded solemnly. '*Big* trouble.'

I believed her – she was so sweet and kind-looking, I couldn't bear the thought she might suffer on my behalf, so I looked down and gritted my teeth.

'Okay,' I said. 'I'll eat something, I'll do it.'

It nearly killed me, tasting the buttery saltiness of the toast and the thickness of the shake, but I managed to eat half a slice and drink half a glassful of the vanilla stuff. That was it – I couldn't manage any more.

As I sat back, explaining that I'd done my best for her, granny nurse cracked a wide, smug smile. SHE'D LIED! I realised then she had tricked me into eating and, all of a sudden, I felt so angry and stupid for falling for it. She whipped the tray away while I lay there, seething, and now I had no choice: I had to lie in bed with nothing to do but think how foolish and weak I'd been for letting myself eat.

The constant presence of the nurses now began to grate on me. Even in the bath, they stayed with me. For the most part, they were considerate and didn't stare, though I was still horribly embarrassed. The only nurse I really bonded with was a lady called Andrea. The first time she took me for a bath, she offered me a cigarette. I was blown away as I was nowhere near the weight required – but I took it anyway.

'Why are you doing this?' I asked (my defences were always up in this place).

'I'd like a smoke myself,' she replied nonchalantly, helping herself to one, too. 'And no one needs to know.'

Andrea would chat to me about her life while I enjoyed the relief of feeling the warm, bubbly water. I'd cover myself in bubble-bath foam so she couldn't see anything, and the water seemed to give my aching body some respite. Andrea was in her late twenties, single and had long, fair hair. She was really open with me and talked about everything from parents to boyfriends. I always looked forward to our bath-time chats.

But it wasn't always Andrea or Fiona with me – a lot of the time the nurses were strangers, student nurses, since Ninewells, where I was being treated, was a teaching hospital. They'd come and go, and I had no idea who would be on duty with me from one hour to the next. Eventually, after two weeks of being constantly shadowed, I was so pissed off, I decided there was nothing else for it: I had to eat, just to get them away from me. So each mealtime, I'd nibble at whatever they put in front of me. I hated it, of course, it was like torture, and seeing the weight start to go back on was agonising, but the pay-offs did help. An hour of radio, some magazines, the chance to write – it all helped to relieve the boredom and allowed me to focus on something other than my illness.

The only problem now was my uncooperative bowels. It had been over 10 days since I'd had a movement and I put this down to the fact that I was too embarrassed to poo in front of any of the nurses, even Fiona. At first, the pain in my stomach came and went without me really noticing – after all, I was used to putting up with pain. But one night, I woke up in agony – my stomach was killing me – and screamed out to the nurses for help.

Sister came and examined my stomach, or at least she tried to, as I couldn't move without a searing hot pain shooting up my whole body. I was sweating now and crying with distress.

They pulled the curtain around me and put on the dim overhead light as the ward was in darkness and everyone was asleep. I was trying to cry quietly so as not to disturb the others but it was very difficult.

'We'll have to go against all the rules and give you an enema,' Sister told me. So that's what they did – they laid me on one side, stuck a tube up my anus and tried to flush out the compacted faeces inside me with water. Oh, my God, it felt like I was being pumped up like a balloon! But still nothing came out.

It was now the middle of the night and I was still in such acute pain, they knew they couldn't leave me like this. Fiona bent down and whispered gently in my ear: 'Tina, we're going to have to manually evacuate you. There's really nothing else for it.'

I nodded, mute with horror, pain and anguish. In that moment, I didn't care what they did to me as long as they took the pain away. Lying on my side now, Fiona used her hands inside my back passage. It was the most humiliating moment of my life. If I hadn't been in such distress, I would have died right then from the embarrassment of it all. But even that didn't work.

So now, Fiona left and, moments later, came back with a tray of surgical instruments. I didn't even want to see what she had on there. Still on my side, I felt a pushing and pulling at my anus as she and another nurse worked to remove all the built-up faeces from inside me. I felt sharp little digs of pain followed by a dribbling down my butt and I knew that this was blood. I tried not to think about what was going on and even put my fingers in my ears and hummed music loudly so I could be distracted from the pain and sounds.

But then, all of a sudden, I felt a wave of sickness and started to vomit. Fiona was still working on my bottom but the other nurse ran round now with a bedpan as I puked my guts up, all the while sweating and shaking. Fiona continued emptying me of faeces for about an hour and then cleaned me up, replaced my sheets, and helped me into fresh pyjamas. My stomach felt a bit better but it stung where I was torn around the back passage. I was so relieved when it was finally over but, now, the humiliation overtook me like a tidal wave and I couldn't stop sobbing.

Fiona held me as I wept like a baby.

'I would rather starve to death than go through all that again,' I cried. I could barely look at her, I felt so degraded in that moment. But as ever, she was kind, sympathetic and humane.

'Shush, don't worry, Tina. That won't happen again. You're

okay now and you're going to feel a whole lot better in a few days' time.'

Her kindness was almost too much to bear. *How could she do those things and not hate me*, I wondered. I was full of admiration for her patience, her professionalism, but, best of all, her kindness and understanding. Still, I cried myself to sleep that night. It had been the worst, most humiliating moment of my life and I knew I would never, ever forget it.

Chapter 10

The Psychiatric Ward

The fairy lights twinkled prettily that morning – my first Christmas away from home, Christmas in the psychiatric ward. Already it was a special day – the nurses all wore colourful paper hats, while paper chains and shiny decorations hung around the ward and Father Christmas, whom I recognised as one of the doctors, had distributed small gifts to every bedside. Mine was a little orange teddy bear, which I hugged close to me as I waited for my family.

It was Celine I saw first – she came sprinting towards me with a huge grin on her face and I almost squealed with delight as she flung herself at me, giving me a great big hug. The others came in behind her, each wearing warm, happy smiles. It was so good to see them after all this time and I scooted over in bed to let Celine cosy up beside me. It felt so nice to feel her next to me, smell her clean hair. I'd missed her and the others so much.

Mum and Dad were together, looking to the entire world like perfect, happy parents. Not the people they had actually become.

'How are you, honey?' Dad asked. 'You feeling okay?'

'Are you getting better?' Celine jumped in. 'Are you coming home soon?'

'Yes, I'm fine,' I said, grinning at her. 'I'm getting better every day.' It was a lie, of course – I was eating again, it's true, but only the tiniest amounts, and if my vegetables were covered in creamy, cheesy sauce, I always scraped it off. I hadn't put on enough weight to get visitors, but for Christmas, the ward made an exception.

'Are you okay?' I asked my sisters. I felt so guilty for being in here, for abandoning them to their miserable lives.

'Yeah, we're all good,' replied Sophie. At that moment, the lady in the bed opposite us started crying – loudly. Everyone turned to look at her and, for a minute, I was filled with panic – I didn't want my family to be upset today.

'Oh, don't mind her,' I said casually. 'She's fine. Tell me, what have you lot been up to? Celine, have you been doing your homework? Are you going to visit Granny in the holidays?'

We talked for about an hour before they left to get back for their Christmas dinner. I was so pleased they had all come, and it seemed Mum and Dad had made a special effort to be nice to each other today. Secretly, I was glad not to be at home this Christmas. The ward was jolly that day, with everyone singing carols – it was a world away from the depressing little flat I had come to hate.

It was another couple of weeks before my weight was up

enough for me to be allowed to get up out of bed and go to the toilet on my own. Freedom! On that first day, I was up and down to the toilet like a yo-yo – just for the sheer hell of it! Now, for the first time, I could start to meet some of the others on my ward. I met Pam, first – she was the lady with the baby who had come shuffling towards me in her slippers like a zombie on that first morning. Pam was in the side room just across the ward, and she had severe postnatal depression. Her baby, Emma, would cry for hours and Pam would just ignore her. It made me feel so sad, hearing that baby crying and crying – the nurses were in with her a lot.

I could see Pam and the baby from my bed. At first, Pam didn't speak much because she was on a lot of medication but, over time, we began to chat. She told me that the depression made her hear voices that told her that if she didn't do things a certain way, the baby would die. I was horrified when she told me she'd been put in the hospital because of an overwhelming urge to kill herself and hurt her child. It was horrible and I felt so sorry for her. She didn't seem to have a bond with her baby at all. I myself was dying to pick Emma up – she was beautiful, the most adorable creature I'd ever seen – but I was now so weak, I was frightened I might drop her.

In January 1986, furious blizzards swirled outside our windows but, in Ward 18, we were protected from the elements. In here, we were safe and snug, cocooned from the weather, the real world and all its hardships. But I was missing exercise and as soon as I was allowed to walk around, I set myself little routines. I would go to the concourse and run all the way back every day, then I would try to run up and down the three sets of stairs as quietly as I could but as fast as I could, too. It felt great to get back moving around again. My muscles had been eaten up by my own body for survival and now I had nothing left so I had to start building up all of my strength again.

It didn't take long for me to spot two other girls who I guessed were also in there for anorexia. Both super-thin, to me they looked amazing. They introduced themselves as Violet and Marie. Violet was the one who impressed me most – her clothes were beautiful, all colour-coordinated, her hair was gorgeous and groomed and she had this amazing air of self-possession. I thought she was stunning.

'Where do you get your clothes?' I breathed, eyeing the beautiful navy wool polo neck she wore that day.

'Benetton,' she replied.

Marie was about eighteen and really pretty, too, with very dark, curly hair. I thought they both looked great – thin and beautiful, they seemed so in control. They were long-term eating-disorder sufferers, they explained, and had been in and out of the ward for months and months. Talking to them was brilliant. They gave me lots of tricks and tips to keep my weight off without actually eating and avoiding falling below the 8 stone mark, where I was put back to bed and kept with a nurse.

'You've got to drink the Build Ups,' Marie explained. 'If you drink them, then you can still maintain your weight without actually eating.'

We chatted for hours. These girls were just like me, apart from being much more knowledgeable about the condition. They both made themselves sick – a condition called bulimia – but I told them that I hated making myself sick. Violet was an only child with two very successful parents – her dad had bought her a car for her birthday, which frankly blew my mind.

'You're so lucky!' I exclaimed.

'Oh, sure,' she replied drily. 'It's amazing what guilt can do.'

Obviously, Violet wasn't happy at home but I didn't push her to talk about her issues. Like me, they were both fiercely private people and I guessed, like me, they weren't really interested in showing their weaknesses. No, instead, we plotted and planned how to foil the hospital's attempts to cure us.

'What are the drugs?' I asked them.

'Oh, that's Chlorpromazine,' Violet explained. 'It's a very strong anti-psychotic drug, which makes you drowsy. And they give us Dothiepin, too, which is an anti-depressant. They use them to turn us all into zombies and make us easier to control!'

At this, Marie shoved her arms straight out in front of her, let her mouth go slack and rolled her eyes around in her head, imitating a zombie. We all laughed. Violet was really smart, with a whip-sharp wit – she was even taking a degree while in hospital. I admired her greatly. I was ashamed that my illness had caused me to miss so much of school; consequently, I had no grades or qualifications whatsoever. However, when they told me that, at 16 years old, I was the youngest anorexic they had ever seen on the ward, I felt oddly proud.

We were all on the same treatment plan and the only difference was the start weight and end weight as we were all different heights. It didn't matter – we all felt the same: too fat. If we met up for chats, we would always do so standing up so we could burn more calories – as it was, I hated sitting on the blue plastic chairs, where I would look down at my thunder thighs and see them spreading out on the seat under me.

It didn't take long for me to put my new plan into action. That night, I hid a polystyrene cup in the bottom of the bin in the last toilet cubicle. The next morning, just before my weigh in, I went to the toilet. There, I retrieved the cup and, as quickly as I could, gulped down 10 cups of tap water. I could literally feel the water sloshing around inside me – if I drank any more, I would probably have thrown up. This time, when I went to the weigh chair, I pulled my feet in under me as Violet and Marie had instructed (it helped, they said, to bring your weight up). I was thrilled when my weight came in at 7 stone 8 lb – what a result! The nurse on duty with me was delighted and told me I was free to have my family visit.

From that day, my family all came to visit at different times. My granny Lana was especially pleased to be able to see me – we'd walk the concourse together and she would put her thumb and forefinger round my wrists to see how skinny they were. Then she would cry.

'We all miss you so much,' she said, wiping away the tears. 'We just want you to get better soon so you can come home again.'

It was so sad to see her upset like this and I hated the fact that it was all my fault.

One day, I got an unexpected visit from my cousin Marco and one of his friends. We went up to the concourse and they bought me a glorious can of Diet Pepsi, my favourite. As I was drinking it, I was very aware of the boys staring at my hand holding the can, so I stopped drinking.

'What's wrong?' I asked.

They exchanged worried looks and then Marco said: 'Tina, your hands look like a skeleton.' I just laughed – *if they could only see the rest of me!* They never mentioned it again and I didn't let it ruin my afternoon – I was just glad for the company.

Visits from my parents were nice but they never came at the same time. I had an inkling they were trying to keep things from me because our conversations were always light and untainted by news of rows or disagreements. Unlike at home, Mum didn't complain about my dad once. It was my new friend Violet who told me what was going on.

'The doctors tell them not to say anything to you that might upset you,' she explained after one visit from my dad where he brushed aside all my concerns about my sisters with a breeziness that didn't quite ring true.

'It's part of the recovery process,' she went on. 'Negative stuff isn't welcome here, so don't be surprised if you're fed a lot of bullshit from your family. God knows, mine never talk about anything important at all!'

It annoyed me slightly, knowing they were putting on a front for me, but I couldn't help but feel grateful at the same time. I'd been dealing with their mess for so long, I was glad of a break from the fights and conflict.

One early evening, Mum came to see me and we sat together in the dining room where, at this time of the day, the staff always left out baskets of toast dripping with butter for anyone feeling peckish. Naturally, I wasn't interested in the food but Mum's eyes kept sliding over to the baskets. Eventually, she suggested we have some toast together.

111

'No, thanks, Mum,' I said. 'I've just eaten.'

I think by now she had heard every excuse in the book and perhaps this time, it was just the last straw.

'Oh, for God's sake!' she exploded. 'Will you just eat something?'

I looked at her blankly – did she really think this was going to persuade me?

'Look, either you eat this toast or . . .' she hesitated, '. . . or, I swear, I'll become anorexic, too!'

I nearly laughed out loud at this – as if it was simply a matter of choosing! She knew nothing about it, nothing at all. I was so tickled by this idea that I taunted her: 'Okay, go on then – become anorexic!'

I sat there smirking as she puffed out her cheeks, clearly vexed. She couldn't take the control away from me that easily. I didn't care how frustrated she was – frankly, I didn't feel anything much towards my mum in those days and I loved the idea that she was going to try to be an anorexic. She changed the subject and after five minutes picked up a slice of toast and started munching on it.

'Oh, well, that lasted a long time,' I muttered sarcastically. Mum shot me a look – then she wiped the crumbs from her smart pencil skirt and pushed back her long blonde locks.

By now, I was getting daily counselling and therapy sessions from a host of different doctors. Dr Ballinger was my psychiatrist and she was lovely – small, with red, curly hair. She was very ruddy and outdoorsy – always talking about going on long country walks. Euan was the cognitive behavioural therapist – his sessions were always my favourite. He'd draw little pictures of plates of food and then a picture of me with bubbles coming out of my head, to try to get an idea of my thoughts and feelings around food. He'd try to replace these negative thoughts with positive ones. I did try hard to take on board what he said but it wasn't always so easy to put it into practice.

Sometimes I just chatted to the nurses.

Michelle, one of the regulars, sat down with me one day and asked what I thought of the illness.

'It feels like it's enveloping me,' I told her, and she nodded. She had short blonde hair pushed back over her ears and a keen, honest face. 'It gives me some control because everything at home has gone wrong. But I don't like the fact that it keeps me away from my sisters. If it weren't for me, they would be left alone all the time – they're everything to me.'

Michelle nodded again, then put her head to one side, resting on her fingers: 'You know, Tina, you're a textbook anorexic. You've got to stop worrying about your sisters because they're never going to appreciate what you've done for them.'

Now that made my blood boil – who the hell was she to tell me about my own flesh and blood? I knew my sisters loved and appreciated me – of course they did. And being called a 'textbook anorexic' wasn't all that nice either. Nobody wants to be textbook anything. I wanted to be different, special – I'd set out to be the best anorexic in the world and it irked me that she could dismiss this by lumping me together with everyone else.

Now the days slid into weeks, which slipped into months and the trees outside our windows budded with the promise of spring. Every day, I drank the Build Ups but kept my eating to a minimum. As a result, my weight slipped back under 7 stone

5 lb and I was once more confined to bed, with a nurse by my side. All meals were to be eaten in bed, no visits. It was hell and made me more determined to get out of there. So I upped my food intake and tried not to exercise too much. Now I was just focused on one goal – getting out.

By the beginning of June, I was well enough to have day outings and I begged the hospital to let me go home. It was very strange returning to the flat. Instantly, I was filled with guilt for my sisters, as I had not been there for them. I felt they needed me and that I was a failure as, once again, my selfishness prevailed with my eating issues. It was almost a relief to go back to the ward after these visits. There I could feel safe and secure and hide from my family's problems.

One afternoon at the end of the July, I waited anxiously for my turn to be called to see the doctors. Discharge day was a big deal on the ward and it was always a nerve-wracking time – the lucky ones would fly out of the room and literally race to get their things before fleeing out of the door. It was almost comic, the way they would be so elated to leave, like prisoners being set free.

This day, I knew I had a good chance: I'd maintained my goal weight for three whole weeks now and I'd acted like the model patient. At 3 p.m., Michelle came to get me, to show me into the room where Dr Ballinger sat with a panel of three others, most of whom I knew from my seven months on the ward.

Dr Ballinger was smiling broadly.

'Well, we think you're doing really well, Tina,' she said. 'I can see here that your weight is stable and you've been making very good progress in your counselling sessions. I think you're ready to be discharged.'

Yippee! I nearly leapt from my seat right that minute – it took enormous will not to just run out of there, like a madwoman! But I waited until the meeting was over, thanked the doctors and then dashed to my bed. My bag was already packed so I just said goodbye to Pam, Fiona and Violet and ran all the way up the stairs, out of the main hospital entrance to catch a bus home. All the way back, I couldn't help but grin to myself like an idiot. It had been six long, torturous months away from my family, from my life, and I was so excited to be free again. Mum knew to expect me as the ward had called ahead.

I let myself in the front door with my key and, almost straight away, I felt the coldness of the flat, the bleakness, overtake me. It wasn't warm or homely.

'Tina!' Mum exclaimed, walking through from the kitchen. She seemed so happy to see me but, in that moment, I didn't want her to touch me. As she pulled me to her in an embrace, I just stood there, arms locked to my sides, unable to hug her back. I put my things down in the hallway and walked around the flat, looking at everything as if in a dream. *Was this my life?* I wondered as I picked my way through the mess that my sisters had left behind that morning. Old dresses and socks lay about the floor, schoolbooks and drawings were scattered on the dining-room table. In my room, I examined the Madonna and U2 posters on the walls.

It all came flooding back to me then – the misery that had led to my being in hospital all that time. And, for some reason, I couldn't hold it back – it washed over me like a tide.

When my sisters all got home from school, they rushed to greet me and covered me in hugs. Half an hour later, when they were sprawled out in front of the TV, munching on toast, I quietly took myself off to my bedroom and started exercising again.

Chapter 11

Relapse

Life at home had not changed. And neither had I. If anything, my anorexic urges were stronger than they had ever been. I embraced the anorexia and the strength and control it gave me with renewed determination and zeal. We had been separated for too long and now I raced back towards it, like a child looking for the safety of its mother.

Mum and Dad never spoke any more – if we ever saw Dad it was when he came to the house on the Sunday morning after a failed meet-up the day before when us girls, like four lost little orphans, would sit and wait for him all day long. He was working, he'd say, he couldn't get away. He was full of remorse – and Mum gave him hell every time – but to me, it didn't matter. We weren't his priority, this much was clear to me. When we did see him, he focused his conversations on the younger ones and that was fine with me – my goal now was to get to 4 stone and I didn't want anyone standing in my way.

At first, I did all the things I was meant to – I attended my Psychiatric Outpatients clinic with Dr Ballinger, or 'Pissed Off People clinic' as we used to call it. I kept up with the nurses, regularly calling in to give them my weight but, as time went on, I stopped. After all, the weight was falling off me in record time and if they knew the truth, I knew they would call me in.

I stopped eating the day I was discharged and though Mum would beg me to eat and I caught the concerned looks in my sister's eyes, I wasn't about to be deterred; I simply stopped looking in their eyes. I had boundless energy, more than ever, and I was totally in control. I was so nutritionally well from the eating at the ward, I felt healthy and I thought I understood my body, my brain and illness better than anyone else. I prided myself on being an 'anorexia expert'.

Now I ran all the time and I set myself a target of 1,000 sit-ups and push-ups a day. I was back in Boots, weighing myself every day and loving it. Within two months, I was down to 5 stone 10 lb, the lightest I had ever been. But I knew I could go further, and I would. The weight hadn't been on me long enough in hospital to stay on and I was excited by the thought of how easy it was for me now to lose weight again. Every day that passed, I got thinner and thinner, and though I could hear Mum pleading with me to call the hospital, I knew I was fine.

By the time I reached 5 stone, I could barely walk. My whole body ached as never before. My back killed me, my stomach was in agony, but this is what I expected – I knew I had to push through the pain and never give up. Giving up was a weakness and I was stronger than I had been my whole life!

Except, as the pounds fell away, my strength seemed to desert me, too – now I struggled to complete 50 push-ups and 50 sit-ups a day. It was maddening! But I knew I could do it, if I just pushed myself harder, so I'd stay awake half the night, trying desperately to meet my targets.

One night I had set myself a target of 500 push-ups and I had 150 left to do. My heart was pounding out of my chest and all my energy was spent, but still, I refused to give up. I would do this push-up if it bloody well killed me! My arms cried out in pain as I flattened my palms against the floor and braced to take the strain before launching myself upwards with an almighty heave. As I did so, my head just melted away. The next thing I knew, I came to on the carpet. I was furious that I'd allowed myself to faint – so, in defiance of my weak body, I carried on until I hit my target of 150.

The effort was unbearable – but I pushed on, cursing myself in my head. *Come on, you fat, lazy slob! Come on, you weak little shit! You're nothing – you're revolting, you can't even do the easiest thing. Now push, PUSH!* At that moment, the only thing that would have stopped me from finishing those push-ups was death. And that didn't frighten me in the least. Finally, after an agonising two hours, I made it to 150 and promptly rushed to the toilet to throw up with exhaustion.

The following week, I was in my room, arranging my weight printouts from Boots, carefully smoothing down any folds and marvelling at how all the numbers tumbled downwards to my newest weight of 5 stone, when Mum called out from the corridor.

'It's Sister Cummings on the phone for you, Tina!'

'Tell her I'm busy!' I hollered back. 'I'll call her tomorrow.'

'Tell her yourself,' Mum said, putting her head around my door and holding the phone out to me. I was angry for being interrupted in this way – she hadn't even knocked!

'Hi, Sister,' I started, keeping my voice friendly and even. I knew she was going to be mad with me for I hadn't called my weight in for weeks.

'Tina, we need to know why you haven't been in touch,' she said, crossly.

'I haven't called because I'm fine,' I insisted. 'I'll give you a ring when I need your help, but I'm fine for now.'

'Tina, how much do you weigh?'

'I'm 5 stone, Sister.'

I could have lied, I knew that, but I didn't want to – I wanted to show off. Inside, I was proud to have achieved such a dramatic weight loss so quickly. I caught the sharp intake of breath on the other end of the line, the momentary pause as I sensed Sister Cummings trying to compose herself. Even so, when she spoke, her voice, though low and controlled, was fizzing with anger.

'Tina, you need to get into hospital right away or you will *die*,' she told me.

'I don't care,' I retorted. 'I don't care and, anyway, I think you're lying to me again – I'm not going to die.'

'Tina, you are dying *now*! Right now! You must come in so we can check you over and make sure you are not going to be in pain.'

It was those last few words that got to me – she wanted to make sure that I wouldn't be in pain for my last days on earth. That made sense to me. I knew I didn't want to die at home, with my sisters around me – after everything they had suffered already in their young lives, I couldn't put them through that. I didn't want to live any more, it was true, but I didn't want to die an agonising death either. For the first time, I felt a little shiver of fear creep up my spine as I considered that these were probably my final days. For what no one knew was that I had also stopped taking in fluids the day before. Now, it was only a matter of days.

Once I had put the phone down, I asked Mum to take me to the hospital. Now that I had let myself see the truth, I wanted to ensure that the end was peaceful, not painful. Every inch of my body was crying out in agony and I was so weak, I could barely put one foot in front of the other. Mum called Dad and told him to meet us there. The ward sent an ambulance and, by the time we got there, I was practically crawling on my bony knees as I had nothing left. I wouldn't fight any more, I couldn't – I had admitted the truth to myself and now I was resigned to dying. All my energy was gone and I felt like I was finished.

My legs gave way once I arrived and I collapsed onto the ward floor at the side of the bed I had been in the last time. When I came to I felt a tremendous sadness sweep over me – I truly hoped I wouldn't wake up again. I wanted to die now, more than anything else. Somebody helped me onto the bed and I lay there for a few minutes before something inside me snapped and I realised I had been tricked again: they just wanted to make me fat!

The power of my fury propelled me upwards and I sat up and started screaming: 'Get me out of this fucking bed! I want to go home, take me home now!'

My parents were nowhere to be seen but Sister Cummings

came rushing over, to try to calm me down: 'Hush now, Tina, you really need to be lying down! You're not well enough to go home – you're very, very sick.'

'You fucking liar!' I spat. I'd never been so rude to anyone in my life before – it was as if I was possessed. But I couldn't stop.

'There's nothing wrong with *me*!' I shrieked. 'You're just lying to me to keep me here. Well, nothing's going to stop me – I'll take myself home.'

And with that, I threw myself out of bed, tried to walk to my little cabinet for some clothes, but fell over. My legs had completely given up and I was dragging myself around to get dressed. I was crying hysterically now and the next thing, Dr Ballinger appeared and tried to reason with me to stay.

'Tina,' she said. 'Look at me, Tina – you know you need to be here. Come on, you've been here before. It's fine. We're going to take care of this.'

But I just lay on the floor, weeping and screaming to go home. I felt hands on my arms as the nurses tried to lift me back into bed, but I lashed out at them, kicking and screaming.

'GET OFF ME! GET THE FUCK OFF ME!'

WHO THE FUCK WERE THEY TO TRY TO STOP ME? I was furious for allowing myself to be tricked again. I felt rage – RAGE! RAGE! *RAGE!* and I didn't know where it was coming from or how to stop it. Every cell in my body was clenched and fighting for survival – I *had* to get out of there.

I passed out again and, when I came to, I noticed they had put a tube up my nose while I was unconscious.

'What the hell is this?' I fumed. 'Take this out this minute – you're not going to feed me through a bloody tube! TAKE IT

OUT NOW OR SO HELP ME, I'LL PULL THE THING OUT MYSELF!'

Fiona stood by my bedside, real concern in her eyes.

'We can't take it out, Tina,' she told me gently. 'You need to have it because you're very sick.'

At that point, I went mad. I pulled the damn thing right out of my nose and threw it on the floor. Once again, I tore my covers off and tried to sit up – this time, I really was going to leave and there was nothing they could do to stop me.

'Please, please calm down,' Fiona begged. 'You're very sick, Tina – your heart is very weak, as are your kidneys and liver.'

But I just laughed in her face.

'You're talking shit!' I shrieked. 'You're just lying to me to keep me here!'

I didn't believe a word any of them said any more. Nothing was making sense in my head; it was very blurry. But I was right, I knew that, they were all lying, conniving bastards! Fiona looked a little hurt but she didn't move. Instead, several other nurses came to the bedside and held me down – I felt a prickle along my arm and I saw one of the doctors was giving me an injection. *What's happening? What are they doing to me?*

Moments later, a strange man in a black suit appeared with a big leather-bound folder. He looked like an accountant or a lawyer.

He asked me if I wanted to leave.

'Of course I fucking do!' I screamed at him.

'Well, I'm afraid we can't allow that. We are sectioning you under the Mental Health Act . . .'

At that point, all the fight went out of me. I felt my body

relax as I realised that I had lost – they were keeping me there and there was nothing I could do about it. Somewhere, far off in the distance, I could hear the man's voice prattling on about legalities, reading me a load of jargon that I neither heard nor understood.

Confused and despairing, I begged them to let me leave.

'Please, Fiona, *please* just let me go now! I don't want to be here,' I wept. But it was out of her hands. I heard the words 'court order' and I realised this was serious; I was terrified. Now they had control over me and they could do what they wanted, administer anything at all, for my own safety.

Finally, the strange man told me that the police could arrest me if I tried to leave the premises.

'Fuck you!' I said to the man as he turned to leave. *How dare they! How fucking dare they keep me as a prisoner like this! It was outrageous, disgusting!*

Now, Fiona sat at one side of the bed and Sister Cummings sat at the other, talking very quietly and calmly to me.

'You are the sickest you have ever been,' Sister Cummings said. 'You will die unless we keep you here.'

'But I don't care,' I sobbed. 'I want to die. I don't care any more – I've had enough.' The adrenalin was gone, as was every last drop of energy I had left in me. By now, I was a lot calmer; the injection must have kicked in and I let Fiona put the tube back up my nose. It was horrible.

'Okay, now, Tina, you need to pass urine so we can check your kidneys. And we also need to take a blood sample to run some tests.'

I offered my arm for the syringe, knowing I had no choice

any more. But every time the needle went in and Fiona drew on the syringe, it would snap back into the empty barrel. It was very painful, especially since my skin was now so tight that it broke and bled every time the needle went in.

'We can't get any blood, Sister,' I heard Fiona tell Sister Cummings.

'I haven't had fluids in two days,' I said weakly.

Sister Cummings wasn't angry any more – her face was a picture of sorrow and pity. I could see now that she really did care about me but still they couldn't get any blood out of my arm, not a single drop. Somewhere deep inside, I felt a satisfied sense of a job well done – success!

Finally, I had achieved the emptiness I had sought for so long.

Chapter 12

Praying for Death

That night, I slept like a baby but, when I woke up, I was consumed with despair. *Why won't they just let me die? Why won't they just let me go in peace?* From the moment I opened my eyes that morning, I was pushed and pulled around as the nurses and doctors fought to save my life.

First, they hooked me up to a catheter – now that I was getting fluids through the tube, I needed to go to the toilet but a bedpan proved useless. Nothing was coming out of me. My kidneys weren't working properly any more as my body was desperately trying to hang on to every last drop. So Fiona fitted the catheter. It seemed to take for ever and was horribly painful.

'I'm sorry, Tina,' she whispered as I cried out in pain. 'All your tubes, veins and arteries have shrunk due to severe dehydration. I'm trying my best not to hurt you.'

When it was finally in place, another nurse tried to put a

cannula in the back of my hand – more agony as my veins kept collapsing. After half an hour of this, she gave up. Minutes later, another nurse appeared, wheeling in a heart monitor, to which she hooked me up with chest pads. So now I really was on life-support – liquid foods, catheter, heart monitor. Desperate to tell them to stop, to just let me go quietly, I didn't have any control any more: I was sectioned.

Worried-looking doctors streamed past by my bed now at regular intervals, talking in hushed tones, checking my charts and conferring over my treatment. I gave them all baleful looks. *Look what you've done to me!* I wanted to shout. *Look what you've turned me into! I'm a person, not a machine, and I just want to die in dignity and peace. Why won't you all just leave me be?*

Astonishingly, food was brought to my bedside. It felt like a sick joke – they knew they couldn't get me to eat this stuff. They must have seen I was determined to die, no matter what. My anger was as strong as ever, but sedated now. I couldn't move a muscle so I just lay there, waiting and praying for death. Day became night, and night bled into day again – how long had I been there? I didn't know.

Now they brought the weigh chair to my bedside as I couldn't get up and, since I was only being drip-fed a liquid diet, the weight continued to fall off. They refused to tell me how much I weighed now, knowing the low numbers only fuelled my determination, but I was an expert, of course, and I could read the scales even when lying down. For every pound that disappeared, I cheered silently inside my head. I was 4 stone 11, then 4 stone 10, 4 stone 9 . . .

Around two weeks after being sectioned, my tongue went

completely black from a fungal infection due to anaemia. I was given jelly lozenges to try to get rid of it and, though I hated the thought of anything passing my lips, I was disturbed enough by the weird change to take them. My teeth were already a mess but now I developed terrible toothache lying there in bed. But since I was too ill to be moved, they couldn't get me to a dentist, so they just gave me pain relief.

The sedatives they gave me were so strong I slid in and out of consciousness, barely able to keep a hold of myself for a few minutes. The lights would dim, my body relaxed and I'd slip into dreamy unconsciousness, welcoming the opportunity to let reality fade away. All I knew, when I came round from another dozy sleep, was that I wanted to die: *I WANT TO DIE!* At 4 stone, I could barely hold a thought in my head, let alone move, and yet that was the only one I clung to.

Where are my family? I wondered one day. *They've abandoned me; they've accepted my decision. It's best I just get on with it and get the job done.* Sadness swept over me – this was for the best. I couldn't hold on any longer – there was not a single part of me that wanted to live. So I just lay there, suspended in a state of limbo, halfway between life and death. I was done. Done.

Except, one morning, I found myself waking to the sound of footsteps. Half asleep still, I felt a strange sense of familiarity. Did I know this person? My eyes slowly opened and I managed to half turn my head, to see my dad standing at the nurses' station.

His voice rang out loud and clear: 'I want to see my daughter!'

'I'm afraid it's not possible, Mr Halford,' the reply came back. 'She's too sick to see anyone. It's really better if you leave now . . .'

I could see my father now and the nurse standing beside him, taking his arm; trying to lead him away from me. At that moment, he turned to look in my direction and, from then on, it seemed as if everything happened in slow motion. He caught sight of me lying in bed, surrounded by tubes and monitors. And, for a moment, I looked into his eyes. Oh, my God, the look on his face was awful!

I had never in my life seen a look like that: terror filled his eyes. There was devastation, anguish, love and hate all on his face. In that second, I could see my father was devastated beyond belief. He put his hand up to his mouth – an involuntary movement that seemed to come from the depths of his soul. He couldn't bear it – he couldn't bear to see me like this and, right then, in that very moment, I saw that this was killing him. *I* was killing him.

Suddenly, a whole pack of nurses surrounded him, taking him by the hands, arms, whatever they could, blocking him from my view, ushering him out of the ward and out of my sight. *Dad!* I wanted to cry out – *Dad! I'm here – I'm here! Don't leave!* But he was gone and I was left with a pain in my heart stronger than anything I'd ever felt in my poor, wrecked body. The sob that came out of me seemed to come from deep within, so hard and fast that it actually made my body scream out in agony. This was unbearable – I was crying and sobbing now, so hard I could scarcely breathe. I gasped and gasped – drinking in the air with desperation, like a diver coming up to the surface of the sea. I wanted to live now. I wanted to live *so* much! I couldn't put my father through this pain any longer; I knew that now.

Dad had been determined to see me. He had defied all the doctors' orders, he had fought the nurses, and he'd come to see me; he cared about me. Now I knew I would have to eat. Enough was enough – I couldn't break my father's heart any longer. As the tears flowed, I managed to call out: 'Dad! Dad! *Dad!*'

The nurses came rushing over to my bedside, to try to calm me down, but I only wanted one thing now: to see my father.

'He's left,' a nurse told me. 'He's gone.'

No! I felt like an utter failure. I'd failed to make my dad happy, failed to stop them all going through this distress. I couldn't bear the thought of hurting them any more. Sister Cummings came and sat next to me and hugged me. It was what I needed more than anything – to feel the comfort of another human being, to feel love again.

Finally, I stopped crying enough to ask: 'Has anyone else been in to see me?

'Every day,' she said, nodding. 'Every single day for the past three weeks one of your family has either called or been in.'

I was aghast. They all cared! And look what I was doing to them!

'Why didn't you tell me?' I was so confused.

'We have to keep all information from the patients so they can focus wholly on the recovery process,' she explained.

'But I need to know they care!' I insisted, tears filling my eyes once again. 'I didn't realise. I just . . . I just didn't know. Please, *please* will you tell me if anyone calls for me?'

Sister Cummings nodded.

'And please tell them I will be eating from now on, if they

ask,' I added. 'Will you do that? Please? Tell my dad – call my dad now and tell him. The look on his face! Oh, God! Do you think he's okay? I *hope* he's okay. I want you to call him and tell him I'm going to eat again. *Please* – please do it now!'

Sister Cummings knew this was an important moment for me – and I wouldn't take no for an answer. So she got up and picked up the phone at the nurses' station, holding it close to me so I could hear her words.

'Hello, it's Sister here, on the ward. Tina has asked me to call you to make sure you were all right and to let you know she says she is going to start eating as from now.'

That was all I heard and all I needed to hear. That night, I slept better than ever before.

Chapter 13

A Setback

I can't sleep. I'm exhausted – every pore in my being needs to sleep, but something is stopping me. I sigh. And slowly a strange feeling comes over me – a cold, terrifying sense of foreboding and doom. My body goes cold with the sudden surge of terror and my eyes flick open. There, over my head, hanging from the white tiled ceiling I have stared at for weeks, is the shiny blade of a guillotine. A blade. Glinting in the flickering neon lights, teasing me with its sharpness and violence.

I freeze with fear. What do I do? In my panic, I sit bolt upright and look up again. It's still there, hanging between the tiles, threatening at any minute to fall and split me in two. I can almost feel the edge of the blade as it cuts hard and deep into my bones. Now I'm breathing fast, I can't rest, I can't sit back.

'Tina, are you okay? Come on, lie down – you look exhausted.'

Nurses at my bedside – they pull my arm, they try to hold me down, but I can't move. I am rigid, like stone. The blade, I tell them. There is a huge blade there. I can see it, menacingly shining and sharp. Why can't they see it, too?

'There's nothing there.' The voices try to reassure me, they think I'm losing my mind. But it is as real to me as my own hands, now quivering with fear. A long rod is produced — they are poking at the ceiling tiles, just to show me. To prove that there is no blade. But it is hiding. I can tell it is still there and, no, I won't lie back down again. Instead, I crawl to the bottom of my bed and curl up into a small, tight little ball, far from the trajectory of the hanging guillotine.

I don't want to die, I whisper into the silence of this night. I don't want to die . . .

I had started eating the day after Dad's visit, just as I had promised I would. But it was a slow process — at first, I could only manage tiny morsels of food because my stomach had shrunk so much. The nurses marvelled at my sudden appetite, quietly pleased, though unwilling to make a song and dance in case it pushed me to resist them again. I nibbled on little pieces of macaroni cheese, sucked on mashed potatoes and slowly crunched my way through a handful of Rice Krispies. *One bite at a time*, I told myself, forcing myself to chew and swallow as if learning this skill for the first time. Soups were gently sipped, Build Ups drunk and cauliflower cheese approached with extreme caution. At each new meal, I felt like a bomb-disposal expert, trying at once to overcome the fear and panic in my brain with every mouthful but determined to see it through.

But my mind was still in a very strange place. The guillotine episode was as real to me as anything I've ever experienced and, later, when I talked to Dr Ballinger about it, she said it was a hallucination brought on by exhaustion. Now, for the first time, I saw how far I'd slipped from reality. Not just emotionally – my mind was actually tipping over into the point of insanity. It was a terrifying thought; I realised now just how fragile my mind was. All this time, I thought I was perfectly okay – and then, in one second, my mind had snapped. When had that change occurred? I flicked back through my memories to try to pin down when I had lost hold of reality. During all those hours I had spent exercising? The day I decided to stop eating? Or drinking? Or when I had become consumed with fear about eating calories in the air? Maybe this went back to the day in Italy when I'd seen the women gesturing to each other on Rimini beach – or before that? I didn't know. The line between sane and insane was infinitely minuscule and I had clearly crossed it without ever realising.

But I tried to push this thought to the back of my mind as I focused on getting better. Every day, I managed a little bit more food; every day, the scales were brought and my weight rose steadily. Eventually, by November 1986, I'd put on a stone – enough to allow a family visit. I felt a rush of happiness as they all came in to see me, but noted the scared looks in their eyes. I was still very fragile, I knew that, and my skin was paper-thin. They sat around my bed as I questioned them all about school and their lives – here, surrounded by my loved ones, I felt safe.

It became a feature of my world now, this safety I craved: the comfort and the familiarity of the smells, sounds and routines. Each morning, I woke to the scent of linen, soap and baby powder. It was a comforting smell, a smell that made me feel as if I was being cared for. I was well into my teens now but I still used Punch and Judy toothpaste and a princess toothbrush; baby lotion was my preferred moisturiser. In some ways, I felt that here, in the hospital, growing up wasn't a concern for me. Boys and relationships were out – too complicated emotionally. No, here, I could still be a child.

My childhood still held such happy memories – it was a place I could retreat to in my mind, a place that gave me relief from my present circumstances. Thinking about our lives in South Africa reminded me of a simpler time, a time of swimming with my sisters, of running outside together barefoot and screaming with delight, of dancing to *Grease*, playing fetch with the dog. I was fond of my childhood – it was all so much easier than the grown-up world I had been thrust into at thirteen years old. A violent, ugly world I didn't want any part of.

Once my weight was back up to 7 stone, I was allowed out of bed again and, slowly, very slowly this time, I began to move around the ward. But there was no more running for me – I couldn't have run even if I had wanted to, which I didn't any more because I knew that I had to keep the weight on. Now I could take my meals in the dining room and, during the day, I was allowed to wander into the communal areas – the TV room, dining room – where there were male patients, too. They had a separate ward but we shared those two rooms.

Gradually, I started to meet people. Barrie was in his late twenties and very small, with the most amazing blue eyes I had ever seen. Very cute, with a lovely face, he laughed all the time. But not a funny laugh; it was hysterical laughter. His manic eyes never laughed – it was bizarre. The nurses would occasionally bring him into the main TV room and sit either side of him, for security. Whenever I spoke to him, he would just laugh. I never knew how to react to Barry for I had never seen anyone like this before. I didn't feel scared, just confused as to what was going on.

One day, I sat down in the dinner hall next to a man in his late fifties.

'Hi, I'm Tina,' I introduced myself.

'Leslie,' he responded warmly, and held his hand out for me to shake. I chased a potato round my plate with my fork while Leslie chatted amiably.

'I'm here for a rest,' he explained, tucking into the beef casserole he had in front of him. 'About four years ago, God came to me and told me I needed a rest.'

'Oh, right,' I said, nodding encouragingly.

'Yes, She said that I had been working very hard and I needed to come here for a break.'

'God is a lady?' I was curious.

'Oh, yes,' Leslie replied, nodding emphatically. 'Well, She's female – actually, She's an alien. She's lovely though, really lovely! She has told me that in 2000, She's going to come down to earth and collect me in her spaceship.'

'Have you been here four years then?' I was confused – Leslie said God had told him to have a rest four years ago but I hadn't seen him before today.

'Oh, no,' he said, smiling, as if the thought was a preposterous one, 'I only stayed a few weeks that time but, two weeks ago, She came back and told me I needed another rest because I'd been overdoing it. I've been getting ready, you see . . .'

At that, Leslie winked at me confidentially.

'Getting ready for *what*?' I asked.

'For Her arrival, of course! I've been working A LOT on that! You know, building stuff and making things and generally sorting everything out. But She's always watching out for me!' He chuckled to himself then.

'She said I'd made everything so nice for her and she was very, VERY pleased with what I'd done but it was time for another rest, so here I am!' At this, Leslie spread his arms wide, indicating the hospital. 'Just as She planned it!'

We carried on chatting for another half an hour, while I nibbled delicately on the vegetables and drank my Build Up. Eating was still very difficult for me, a real effort, and usually it took a good hour to get a small morsel of food down. I always made sure my mouth was hidden behind my hand as I ate because I was still so self-conscious about eating in front of others, but Leslie was so charming and friendly, he made me feel instantly at ease.

As I walked back to my bed that afternoon, I wondered about him and his story – it all seemed so plausible and, clearly, Leslie believed whole-heartedly in what he was telling me. So who was I to say he was wrong and the doctors were right? It occurred to me then that most of the religious stuff I'd been taught sounded crazy if you really sat down and thought about it. I mean, what was Jesus if He wasn't an alien sent down to change the world? Walking on water, changing water to wine, the feeding of the 5,000 and rising from the dead? I mean, it was all way out there! If Leslie wanted to believe God was a lady alien in a spaceship, who on earth was I or anyone else to tell him otherwise!

Steadily, as the months passed, my weight went up. At mealtimes, the nurses watched me carefully to ensure I was eating enough. The funny thing was, while they were studying me, I was watching them, too. I got to know all the nurses, their shift patterns, their footsteps and who was the most lenient. Since I still craved cigarettes, I used to hide one in my bed and then smoke it late at night. I always knew from the footsteps who was coming and going, how long they stayed for and what direction they were coming from. And I learned to judge when I could light the cigarette and then when to stub it out in some water in a polystyrene cup and throw it in the bin next to my bed.

It was only another month or so before my sectioning was lifted. Now, with my freedom restored, I got out and about and even managed a couple of visits home – I always imagined how lovely it would be to see my sisters but, actually, back in the flat, I never felt happy. Home was a place full of misery and trauma, my memories of it all warped by my illness. Now, the ward was my home and, as nice as it was to see my sisters, I couldn't wait to get back there after each visit. It was as if the walls of the flat would crowd in on me and I felt like I needed to run away.

By July 1987, on the cusp of turning eighteen, my weight was up to a record 8 stone 2 lb, but my depression was at an all-time low. With the weight going back on and anorexia loosening its grip on me, I had no choice but to face the truth about my life. While most of my friends now had boyfriends, were leaving school, starting jobs and generally getting on with their lives, I was stuck in here, suspended between childhood and adulthood. I had no qualifications, no building blocks for my future and my relationship with my family was growing ever more distant. I was so disappointed in myself, at the way I had turned out, and I was clearly a burden on my family. What did I have to look forward to in life? My periods had stopped years ago and, though the doctors reassured me they would return one day, who could say I hadn't harmed my fertility for ever? Could I expect the same as everyone else – a man to love me, children to care for? I didn't think so. Letting go of the anorexia invited in all the unwelcome thoughts that the obsession had kept at bay. My world was flooded with darkness. What was the point of putting on all the weight? What could I possibly hope for after this? Returning to my mum's pokey little flat, only to suffer her and my father's constant disappointment in me? I just could not imagine what would happen to me after I left the hospital. It kept me awake at nights.

One day, I decided enough was enough. First thing in the morning, I stole out of the hospital and visited the local chemist's. I was full of nerves as I asked the lady there for some razor blades for my dad's razor and she guided me to the counter.

After handing over £2.25, I left the shop, still shaking with terror of being found out. Then I ran all the way back to the ward and into the toilet cubicle, where I used to hide my cup for bulking out my body with water. I hadn't done that in ages now – I knew that I was only cheating myself when I cheated the scales.

My heart was pounding out of my chest with adrenalin. I looked around the cubicle – there was a toilet, small sink, tap, mirror and bin. The walls were a depressing grey. It was a dire sight and a horrible realisation to know this would be the last thing I ever saw — a dark, miserable toilet in a hospital.

I stood there, looking at myself in the mirror. Then I started to cry — I cried with disgust at myself, at the mess I'd made of my life. Since that dreadful tap on my shoulder five years ago, before my life had spiralled out of control; I wanted it all to end, I wanted to be happy. To go back to that joyful, innocent time when everything was so simple and easy. But I knew it never would. The tears streamed down my face. No matter what happened to me now, things could never be the same again. My life had cracked the moment my mother had, and I couldn't repair things now. I was damaged; I was at the bottom of a very dark hole and nothing could help me get out. It was hopeless . . .

So I opened the blades. There were six in there, all very shiny and sharp. I had never seen razor blades singly before and was surprised at how sharp and thin they were. As I took one out and held it against my neck, I wondered how to do it. Quickly or slowly? Now I was shaking like a leaf.

Suddenly, I heard someone crying in the next toilet and it made me jump — I was so focused on what I was doing, I hadn't even noticed anyone going in there. The sound brought me into sharp focus. It occurred to me that if I carried out my plan of slitting my throat, the person likely to find me, the one who would hear the thump of my body against the wall and see the blood run out from under the door, would be the woman crying in the next cubicle.

It was an unexpected thought and, for a moment, I wavered. These people were sick enough without me adding to their suffering. How would she cope? What if my suicide prompted another? And what about my family? I couldn't bear to think how distraught they would be when they got the call later to tell them their daughter, granddaughter, big sister was dead. *Tina bled to death in a toilet* – that's what they would have to tell them. How would my little sisters cope with that? A memory, a vision they would carry with them for the rest of their lives, that she killed herself in a dingy hospital toilet.

I can't go through with it. I realised this in an instant – then, in a fit of anger, I sliced straight into my inner arm. The razor sunk easily into my skin and along, about three inches. The skin widened very quickly as the blade was so sharp but I felt no pain – it was like a hot knife in butter. Blood came immediately and I felt very sick – the adrenalin and shock took over and I realised I needed help before I passed out. Already my head was swimming as I felt my hand on the door handle and ran out of the toilet towards the nurses' station. Then I passed out.

When I came to I was on my bed with a big bandage on my arm and the curtains closed around me. Sister Cummings stood by my bedside.

'How long have I been asleep?' I asked.

'An hour – we gave you an injection to keep you calm,' she said.

I was filled with shame, deep shame for what I'd done. 'Please don't tell my parents or sisters,' I begged.

'Of course I won't, Tina. I will leave that one to you to explain as I'm sure they will want to know why there is a huge bandage on your arm.'

She looked at me then, with real sympathy in her blue eyes,

and left me alone, closing the curtain behind her. I closed my eyes again and fell back to sleep.

A few hours later, Sister was by my bedside once again to tell me the doctor was on her way. Now nervousness took hold – how could I explain to her what I did? I didn't even understand it myself.

When Dr Ballinger appeared, she was her usual calm, quiet self. She looked at me with concern but I could hardly meet her eyes, I was so ashamed.

'Hello, Tina,' she said, settling herself into a chair next to my bed. 'How are you feeling?' And she touched my arm with the bandage on it, just very lightly.

The tears sprung immediately to my eyes and I looked down.

'Terrible,' I replied. 'I don't know what happened. I wanted to kill myself, Doctor. I wanted to cut my throat but I couldn't do it – I couldn't put my family through that. I know I'm putting on weight and to everyone else it looks like I'm getting better, but I don't feel any better inside; I feel worse. Worse and worse and worse! I just don't see what my future looks like – I can't imagine it at all. What the hell is wrong with me? Why can't I just be happy and normal again?'

Dr Ballinger listened carefully and when she spoke it was like balm to my troubled soul.

'Tina, you *are* normal,' she assured me. 'Your behaviour today was uncharacteristic of you and it will probably never happen again. This is just a tiny setback and nothing to worry about. You will be happy again with our help. You must trust us to get you there. One day, Tina, you will look back and be surprised that you had this awful illness. I promise you that.'

Setback. I let that word roll around in my head that night. It was a funny word and one used a lot in my time on the ward. Every time I failed to hit my target weight for that week or my mood sunk and I stopped eating, it was described as a setback and I was told not to worry. We were encouraged to look forward, not back – anything that was back was not welcome.

That night, I made a conscious effort to trust the doctors and nurses to help me. Dr Ballinger told me I had a future and so I chose to believe her. I wanted to get better – I didn't want to live with anorexia for ever. Now I knew I couldn't kill myself either, I had no choice – I had to trust them to help me recover.

Chapter 14

Breakthrough

One afternoon, I walked into the smoking room and saw a slim woman with curly, shoulder-length hair in a smart skirt and blouse, perfectly made up. She looked around forty and I assumed she was a new member of staff – there was something swift, efficient and thoughtful about her movements. Her manner was focused and assured, not like many of the patients.

After she stubbed out her cigarette, she said: 'I'm away for a chat with the nurse.'

'Oh, I thought you were a nurse!' I replied, surprised.

'As *if!*' She laughed, then walked off. The next day, I saw her again – looking every bit as immaculate as the day before. She smiled when she recognised me and introduced herself as Lorraine.

Then she asked me why I was in there.

'Guess!' I said, never imagining for a moment she could tell just by looking at me what was wrong.

'Anorexia!' she responded without hesitation, and I had to laugh at myself then for thinking it wasn't obvious.

'I've never been in a place like this before,' Lorraine confided, looking a little scared.

'I've been in and out of here a long time now,' I admitted. 'It's like my second home. It's nothing to worry about. You will be better soon, I'm sure. The staff here are amazing! Why are you here, Lorraine?'

'It's very strange,' she began. 'I had my own business, a catering supplies firm, and it was going great. I'd never run a business before and I thought I'd do my own books for VAT and tax and stuff. Well, after two years, the stress of it all was getting to me and I didn't really know if I was doing it right but, because it was my business, I just had to get on with it.

'One day, out of the blue, I got a visit from the VAT inspector and they went through everything with a fine-toothed comb. After three days of this, I felt like a criminal and incompetent at everything I had worked so hard to achieve. But I carried on. The problem was my confidence was shattered and I questioned everything I was doing. Now I was struggling to grasp the very basics of the work and my mental health began to suffer. I couldn't sleep; I was stressed and upset all the time. I knew I was in a bad place but I didn't realise what was happening until it was too late.'

I nodded as I listened silently. I recognised this thought – so many of us had lost control of our minds without ever knowing it.

Lorraine took a long, thoughtful drag on her cigarette. Then she looked up to the ceiling and blew the smoke upwards, shaking her head as she recalled what happened next.

'A few weeks after the tax inspector's visit, I was walking in town and suddenly a massive black shape appeared in front of me on the pavement and it started swallowing people. I screamed and froze on the spot. A passer-by called 999 and soon a doctor and an ambulance and police arrived. They told me later I had developed psychosis due to the stress and anxiety of the business. I had to give up the business and now I'm on the mend but that was the scariest moment of my life. It was so real to me, Tina, that black thing. And I find it sad that it got to that point before I got help.'

I felt for Lorraine then – she had tried so hard and obviously pushed herself to a point where her mind snapped. It was an eye-opener and showed me once again how easy it is for the human mind to turn on itself.

As the months passed, I made lots of friends on the ward – people with schizophrenia, depression, anxiety, obsessive-compulsive disorders – those suffering all manner of different illnesses. Often I would lie in my bed at night and imagine living inside their heads. It seemed a very scary place to me, probably much darker than I thought mine was. But to them, mine was off-limits, too, for none of them could relate to me, or why I was starving myself to death. Even though I was very ill, I was not scared of my illness as I thought I was always in control and understood my limitations. But you never knew what was going on in other people's heads.

One day, a new lady arrived in the bed next to mine. In

her late twenties, she was quite large and short; she had long, straggly brown hair and scars on her cheeks and forehead from cuts, as well as on her arms and legs. They were the worst self-harming scars I had ever seen in my life. Her forearms were criss-crossed with massive amounts of scar tissue, scar upon scar. They were blue and deep red as well. There were fresh cuts, too, and a lot of dried blood on her chest above her T-shirt.

On the first day, this woman didn't speak to anybody. This was perfectly normal – a lot of people arrived on the ward in a very distressed state and it took them time to settle in. But on day two, she caught my eye while I was listening to a cassette on my Walkman and nodded for me to come and talk to her. She introduced herself as Linda and, as she did so, my eyes flicked down to the terrible cuts and scars on her arms. When I met her eye again, I could tell she'd seen me staring.

'I'm sorry,' I blundered, embarrassed to be caught in this way.

'It's okay,' she said. 'I know it's horrible but it's my only way of dealing with it, you see.'

'Dealing with what?'

'I was raped as a young girl.'

Linda went on to describe in stark, brutal terms how she had been raped. Though I was aware of course that people did horrible things, I had never come across anyone who had been abused in this way before, or at least, not one who wore their scars so openly. Linda's story was shocking and distressing. In the ward, we all had our crosses to bear and this was the place to bear them publicly. If there was anywhere in the world to be open and honest, it was in here. She opened my eyes to a horror

I had never thought about before and I was very sad for her – it made my life look easy in comparison.

'I cut myself because it helps me to get rid of the pain,' she explained. 'The more I bleed, the more the pain comes out.'

As the days passed, I noticed Linda was becoming increasingly unhappy and aggressive in the ward, getting angry and shouting at the nurses. She was cutting herself a lot and always had fresh blood somewhere. During those moments, I would just leave the area – it was quite common for people to have small confrontations every now and again. Besides our problems, each of us could get a little stir crazy sometimes.

But a few days later, I was in the TV room and the next thing all hell broke loose. The sirens started blaring as the emergency panic-alarm button had been pressed. Everyone ran to the top of the ward. I didn't really want to run as I could see the commotion was focused in my bay and I dreaded to look.

Now I heard screams: 'Oh, shit! Oh, Linda, *Linda!*'

Eventually, I got to my bay, from where I saw the most terrible sight I'd ever seen. Linda was standing there, strangling herself with one of my cassette tapes, which she'd unravelled. No longer a healthy pink colour, she was now grey-blue. A second later, she fell to the ground, and all the nurses ran to her and shoved us back towards the TV room. It was terrifying. I curled up in a ball in the TV room, trying to push those images out of my head. At that moment, I started to cry – I just wanted my mum to take me home; I didn't want to be in a place like this any more.

The screams went on a bit longer and then, silence. After an hour, I returned to my bed and Linda was gone, along with everything from her space, including her bed and cabinet. My cassettes too were nowhere to be seen, confiscated by the nurses.

The next day, Sister Cummings told me Linda had been taken to Carstairs, the psychiatric prison, for her own and our safety. At this, I burst out crying and Sister knew exactly why – seeing Linda trying to kill herself like that had been very upsetting.

'Don't worry, Tina, everything will be okay,' she said. 'Linda will be fine.'

But I never found out if Linda was fine. I wondered if a person like her could ever be fine and that made me disgusted with the person who raped her. He had destroyed her life for ever and, even if she managed to get better, she would always carry those terrible scars with her, the physical embodiment of the torture within her soul. We are all such fragile beings, and this person had harmed Linda, probably beyond repair.

But I understood one thing: Linda wasn't trying to hurt or upset any of us – she was only trying to block out the pain that she felt, day in and day out. I understood that perfectly.

It was a constant struggle now to keep the depression at bay. Two months after the incident with the razor, my weight dipped again to 5 stone. I just couldn't face food and starving myself was the one thing that seemed to make me happy. Although I drank the Build Ups, I refused to eat. In truth, I was scared of getting better, of facing the reality of life, of growing up. I was confined to bed once again and visits from my family were cut off. They called the ward regularly to see how I was doing but were not allowed in to see me. And now the black thoughts returned.

You can't do anything right, Tina. You can't even kill yourself properly. You're worthless, a failure and weak! It's time to get the job done now – you've wasted everyone's time and now the best thing to do is just finish it.

I had a plan. Before I was confined to bed, I'd noticed that there was a window on the concourse of the seventh floor with no lock on it (they must have missed it as every other one on every level had full locks). So my plan was to jump. It had been an option in my head for a while and, in some ways, it felt like a little fantasy – this was my get-out plan in case the therapy and counselling failed. Well, it felt like the right time to put it into action. The hours and hours of counselling and therapy hadn't worked – here I was, three years on, still miserable and starving.

I had it all planned. That night, I lay in bed, feeling strangely disembodied. I knew my life would end within hours, I just had to find the right moment to escape. Now I was very calm. As I lay waiting, I began to wonder how it was going to feel, flying . . . As a child I used to imagine, if I was a bird and could fly, what would it feel like? Now I was going to find out and in a weird way the thought made me happy.

I waited until the night staff came on and I saw it was my favourite two nurses. Sister Mary was an older lady, Italian Roman Catholic. She was small, round and loved her job. Every night, she came round to talk to all of us and ask how we were. Never in a hurry when it came to her patients, she genuinely cared about people. I loved it when she was on as she felt like a granny; she would hug me and made me feel loved. She also used to carry little religious cards with either the Virgin Mary or Jesus on the cross on them. She showed them to us and told us we were all loved by Jesus.

Alan, by contrast, was the funny one. He'd bring the Horlicks and coffee to the TV room at night and sit and chat with us all or, if we were bed-bound, he would bring the trolley around the bays. Usually very relaxed, he always had funny anecdotes up his sleeve, which made me laugh – a rare thing on that ward! He treated me like a real person and not just an 'anorexic'; he really lightened the mood. I noticed that people usually behaved better when there was laughter.

That night, just before lights out, Mary came and spoke to me in my bed. She asked how I was doing and listened patiently when I said I'd had a fairly boring day but I was okay, not too bad. I didn't let on just how low I felt.

She showed me a little card with Jesus on the cross, and said: 'God bless you, my child.' Then she kissed my cheek. It broke my heart – this tender, simple act from a beautiful person. I struggled to contain my emotions but, after she left, I started to cry and pulled the cover up over my head so nobody would see. To me, this was the sign that I needed to leave this world. Even though I had no energy and was confined to bed, I now had validation that it was my time to go: the most amazing woman had blessed me. I actually felt like she loved me in some way and she made me feel loved.

Because I knew the pattern of what they did each night, I knew I would not be watched for a few minutes while they locked up the medicine cabinet and turned the lights off. So I waited and, as soon as they left, I dragged my bony frame out of the bed. Instantly, I felt propelled by a huge volt of energy. I ran out of the ward in just my bare feet and nightie, raced up the stairs as fast as I could, my feet slapping the hard, cold floor. My legs and feet ached as there was no muscle there at all and my knees could barely bend. Still, I sprinted up three flights of stairs and then I could see the window across the concourse. My goal was in sight!

Come on, come on!

I urged my body onwards as I knew it was only a matter of seconds now. My heart was pounding; I was nearly free. Then, just feet away from the window, I heard Alan's voice shout: 'TINA, PLEASE STOP!'

I whipped around and they were all running after me: Alan, Mary and two other male nurses. Now I knew I had to get there before they caught up with me and so I tried even harder to run the last few feet even faster – I had to get out of the window and I was not going to fail.

'STOP, TINA!' came their yells. Sister Mary was screaming and screaming. But I just ignored them. Seconds felt like hours as they gained on me. Just as I was about to reach out and touch the handle on the window, I felt the impact of another body on my left side and the momentum slammed us both into the ground with a sickening thud. The pain in my bones hitting the hard floor was excruciating. And the realisation that I had once more failed instantly brought the tears.

It was Alan – he had jumped on me to save me from throwing myself out of the window. I could hardly breathe as I had run so fast and now they surrounded me, all panting hard from running. Sister Mary was very upset.

'I'm sorry,' I wept. 'I'm *so* sorry! I didn't mean to upset you all.'

Alan was hugging me now as I cried and cried. The rest of

them looked dumbstruck as they realised just how close I had come to actually jumping out of the window. The two male nurses put their hands to their foreheads, pushing back their hair and puffing out their cheeks with relief. It had been a close call for all of them, too close.

Alan picked me up and took me back to bed. As I looked back, I saw one of the male nurses place a comforting arm around Sister Mary, whose small frame was shaking. I was put to bed and given more medicine, which made me fall asleep almost instantly.

The next morning when I woke up, I sat up in bed as the nurses busily came past, helping everyone to make their beds. They all said good morning to me but I was too ashamed to look at them.

An hour later, Sister Cummings strode across the ward towards me, holding herself rigidly, obviously furious.

'Well, Tina, are you felling okay this morning?'
But I didn't feel like talking – I just looked down at my hands.

She touched my arm: 'You know you have taken a huge step back and need more help than ever before. Dr Ballinger will be around to see you at 9 a.m.' Then she left.

Dr Ballinger did indeed arrive and explained to me that I had to have new medication and intensive therapy. No visits from my family, either – not until they were happy, she said, even if my weight went up. Now trapped, I was sorry and ashamed for the most part because, although I had been desperate to die in that moment, I actually saw directly how my decision had affected others. Recalling the terror in Sister Mary's eyes, I felt awful, full of remorse.

154

The following evening, when Sister Mary came back on shift, I immediately apologised, weeping with shame.

'You know, Tina, you are precious, as everyone is precious,' she said, looking at me with heartfelt intensity.

As I lay there, week after week, I tried to examine what had got me to this point in my life. Now nineteen, I was on the cusp of adulthood. And yet, after two and a half years, here I was still! How could I go from being a normal child, to smoking drugs, to drinking and having tattoos, to not eating, to nearly dying, to trying to kill myself? What was going on? As I lay there, these thoughts were going round and round in my head. As I reminisced about my life, I felt very sad – I had missed so much. I had ruined all my chances at school; I would never be a dentist or a doctor, I would be nothing. I was not qualified to do anything. How many mountains would I have to climb to become a normal person and get friends and have a normal job?

One night, I lay on my back, staring up at the ceiling, very depressed but, most of all, I was fed up – fed up and tired. I missed just being 'normal'; I hated what I had become. I hated the anorexia so much but it had taken over me like a tsunami; it had saturated my every cell and turned me into a wreck. For the first time, it dawned on me that I was not in control. At first, the thought came like a small whisper in my ear, a whisper from a voice I'd lost so long ago: *You cannot control it. It is controlling you. You are a slave to the anorexia.*

The admission was like a door opening in my mind, and I knew that I had to walk through that door. I thought back to the books I had read years before about anorexia – they never told you about the stuff I was going through. They made it seem quite a small illness, nothing really to worry about. There was no mention of psychiatric wards, of being sectioned against your will; of your excrement being stuck in your body and having to get it incised out — none of that was in there. I felt betrayed and was looking to blame something, *anything*. But, really, I knew that I had no one to blame but myself and only one person could save me.

There and then, I vowed that if I made it through alive, I would make sure I warned others of how bad it can be. I was determined not to be a slave any more, to take back control and get through it. If I managed that, I would be the victor.

The illness is not my friend — that realisation was a breakthrough. And suddenly, I could hear the rational, authentic voice of my own mind telling me something I really needed to hear. And I heard it loud and clear: *Anorexia is not making you happy. All this time, you've been clinging to anorexia as the one thing you think you can control; and yet, all this time, it has been controlling you, killing you.*

One day, I will be normal, I told myself. *Just like Dr Ballinger said. One day, I'll be rid of this illness for ever, but I shan't forget.*

Chapter 15

Healing

'**A**re you kidding me?' My mother was gobsmacked.

'No, I'm serious,' I replied earnestly, a little giddy from the thought of what I had just proposed.

'You want me to bring in *fudge doughnuts* and *purple Quality Street chocolates*?' She sounded like I'd just asked her to boil her own head in a saucepan but, given the history of my eating over the past three years, it was hardly surprising that she reacted with incredulity.

'Seriously?' she asked again. 'You're not having me on?'

'*Mum!*' I laughed then. 'I really do want them – I'm eating again. Look at me! I feel better than I've felt in years. I'm recovering, I swear. And now I want some chocolate, please!'

I could see the clouds of worry pass over her face. Mum was reluctant to let herself be persuaded – after all, I'd assured her I was 'fine' so many times before and I guess she didn't want to allow herself hope, just in case I let her down again. But this time I was determined. More than anything I wanted to be better and, instead of fighting the people around me, I fought the anorexia. The next time my family came in, I looked even healthier – I'd been eating loads and really making good progress with my counselling. My skin was glowing, my hair had come back to life and I knew my smile now was real, not plastered on for the sake of appearances.

'You look great!' my sister Katie remarked, and I could see she meant it.

'Thanks, Katie. You know what? I feel great!'

'Here you go then!' Mum handed over the box of sticky, sugary doughnuts with doubt and uncertainty in her eyes. Would I actually eat them right in front of them? Had I really made that much progress?

I dipped my fingers in and pulled out a plump doughnut, my fingers instantly covered in grains of sugar, and then attacked it with relish. The sweet fried dough gave way to a gooey fudge centre and I felt myself smiling with pleasure. When was the last time they had seen me eat? When was the last time they had seen me eat *like this*? With enjoyment! My mum and sister were open-mouthed with wonder. Within a few minutes, I had polished off two doughnuts and, I have to say, they were the most delicious, amazing things I'd ever tasted. I looked up, grinning at them both, and they were speechless – I hadn't even covered my mouth with my hand!

Anorexia was not going to rule my life, I was determined now; but I even surprised myself, eating those fatty, sugary foods without any problems. However, I realised now that food wasn't the enemy – anorexia was. And any time I started to feel panicky or strange, I'd close my eyes and tell myself: *You are in charge of your own destiny, not the anorexia.*

Within a month, I was up to a very healthy 8 stone 7 lb, my target weight; I was going home at the weekends and doing great. I was also able to have semi-regular conversations and listen to what people said to me. It was a big step – I had been so lonely and isolated by the illness for so long now, my communication skills were bad. Obviously, it would take a long time, but I was definitely on the right track.

There was some discussion between me and the doctors now about leaving the hospital but one thing was clear to all of us – I couldn't go back home. The trauma of my past was too deep and the situation still too fractured for me to cope. On my trips back to the flat, I saw how Katie and Sophie were now in the throes of their troubled teenage years, just as I myself had been, a few years before: there were boys, there was drinking, drugs and fighting. School hardly mattered to either of them and, though I wasn't told all the ins and outs, I got the impression they were just doing their own thing. Mum seemed as impotent to stop them as she had been with me, four years earlier. Celine flitted between my mum and my aunt's house and, meanwhile, Mum, sadly, was as depressed as ever. I felt cut off from it all and, in some ways, though I needed the separation, it made me feel terribly sad – the illness had robbed me of my closeness with my family.

On the cusp of turning twenty, Dr Ballinger booked me into a rehabilitation unit. This was my first step towards independence and, from the first day I visited, I realised it would be perfect.

The unit had lots of bedrooms, each with its own en-suite bathroom. There was a lovely dining room, a games room and secure entry by key only.

The day I left hospital – a sunny July day in 1989 – was strange and a little scary but I knew I was ready for it. I said goodbye to all the patients on the ward and to the doctors and nurses I'd grown to love over the past four years. These people had cared for me, helped me and saved my life on so many occasions. I didn't have the words to thank them, but I tried.

'I don't need you to thank me,' Fiona said, smiling, after we hugged and I apologised for not being able to fully express my gratitude. 'It is enough to see you walking out of here, looking so happy and healthy, and well on your way to recovery. Seeing you succeed and beat your illness makes it all worthwhile. You've done so well, Tina, and we're all very proud of you here. Don't look back now – just keep moving forward. We know you're going to live a very happy life.'

Her words brought tears to my eyes. I thought of all those weeks she'd seen me lying in bed, at death's door, determined to kill myself. And she had never given up – none of them had. Somehow they'd kept the faith with me when I myself had lost all hope. How can you ever thank someone for that? How can you repay them for all the times they told you they believed in you when you didn't believe in yourself? Their words, their love and care, had slowly repaired my troubled soul. All I could do now was prove to them all that I was never going backwards. From now on, it was all about living!

It didn't take me long to settle into the rehabilitation unit – it was full of different people also making the adjustment to the outside world, like me, and there were staff and nurses on hand to support us at all times. I kept up with my therapy every other day and it felt like I was getting better all the time. And I made friends in the unit and began to listen to music and read a lot; I also visited my auntie Annette and my gran everyday. But I didn't run to see them any more – I walked. My body was slowly healing from the trauma it had been through; I had no muscles left so everything had to be rebuilt slowly. My body was shapeless – the rare times I looked at myself in the mirror, I noted that I looked like a malnourished young boy with huge, baggy sweaters draped over me.

I faced one giant hurdle after another. First, I had to accept the re-emergence of my breasts. Before my eating issues kicked in, I had had quite big boobs so I knew, eventually, they would return – and although I dreaded them coming back, when they did, I just went out and bought a bra – I was a woman now and I had to get on with it. Accepting my shape was an inevitable part of my recovery and all those feelings of wanting to regress to childhood were gradually fading; I was on the path to accepting adulthood.

It was scary, but the therapy helped. Every day, I practised reinforcing positive thinking into my brain, replacing the negativity that at one time ruled my every waking moment. The anorexic voice in my head was gradually getting fainter and fainter – and when I heard it, I refused to listen. No, I had to get better and I wasn't going to listen to her destructive, vicious words any longer.

The one part of my therapy that had so far been overlooked was my relationship with my parents. Anorexia is a whole other world

– a very dark, lonely and desolate place, full of doubts and mistrust. You trust nothing and no one so you never want to tell anyone anything. Mum and Dad were now like strangers to me. I did not know what to talk to them about; I had nothing in common with them any more. So I said very little and felt I did not know them.

Kevin, my therapist, said there was a gap to be bridged and explained that he would like to talk to us all together, that it would be beneficial for all of us. I knew we needed this but, at the same time, it was very daunting. My feelings towards them were still so confused – I was angry, full of angst and yet deeply ashamed at the same time. I felt they had let me down and, then, after my anorexia had taken hold, I felt they hated me for putting them through such hell.

Our first session together was strange and tense. Kevin asked Mum to talk to me about how she was feeling.

'I'm really happy with her progress,' she began, choosing her words carefully. 'Tina has missed all her teenage years and it's a terrible thing. I wish I could have changed things. I love her very much. I'm just so thankful that she is moving on. She's an intelligent young lady and I know she'll be fine.'

I was so nervous now, I was shaking – Dad just sat there, nodding his head.

'What else would you like to say to Tina?' continued Kevin, gently.

'I . . . erm . . . I don't know.'

There was a silence then. I cleared my throat and shifted uncomfortably in my seat. Even now, I didn't want to feel I was a burden on them, I didn't want to push them into a difficult situation.

'Okay, well, how has it been without Tina all this time?' Kevin prompted.

'It's been very sad, not having her at home.' Mum's eyes filled with tears. 'I've missed her a lot.'

Dad nodded and then added: 'We were very worried – I thought I was going to lose my daughter.'

The tears were flowing now – I couldn't help it. It was such a relief to hear them say that they loved and missed me. I could see there was no anger there at all, just love. I didn't say much myself – I wanted to apologise but at the same time I was eager to tell them how much they had both hurt me. But I couldn't – I couldn't cause them any more pain. I was so conflicted after all this time and. though I knew this was an important part of the healing process, I needed time to disentangle my feelings towards them.

Two weeks later, Dad and I had a session on our own. I told him about the time he tried to see me, when I was 4 stone, and how it had been his determination to make contact and then the horror on his face when he saw me in bed that had made me want to get better. The moment I told him, I could see he recalled that day as vividly as I did.

'Oh, Tina, I couldn't believe it!' he said, shaking his head and wiping away the tears. 'To see you like that, it was awful. And the worst thing about it was, I couldn't understand, I just couldn't make sense of it. Why were you doing that to yourself? None of it was your fault! Everything that had happened between your mother and I – I know it was hard for you girls, but you were punishing yourself and I couldn't bear that. It was *me*, I was to blame! All those times I didn't show up – I'm so sorry. I know it affected you and, then, before I knew it, you were *dying*! You were dying right in front of our eyes and I didn't know how to help you, none of us did. And I wanted to. So much. I wanted to put it right again.'

I couldn't look at him now – it was hard to hear but I knew it was good for me. For the first time, my father was opening up to me, talking about the giant hole that had ripped through all our lives; apologising for the times he let my sisters and me down. It was what I needed to hear but, at the same time, I couldn't bear him carrying this guilt around.

'I didn't understand it either, Dad,' I tried to reassure him. 'But you did help. You came and you showed me that you cared – it made a difference.'

For the first time in years, the barriers between my parents and me were breaking down. At last, we were all mending.

Sadly, my sisters were now out of reach. During my time in hospital, I had only seen them when my parents brought them in so, for four years, we had had very little communication. I would spend hours worrying about them. It broke my heart that I had left them alone to survive in the toxic atmosphere at home as I felt they were my responsibility. It took many hours of counselling to understand that I had blamed myself for the divorce and only after I had accepted that it was not my fault could I fully recover.

So I tried – I saw as much of Katie, Sophie and Celine as possible, but now they were dealing with their own issues. Celine was doing well at school but I could see she was upset by the fact that she rarely saw Mum and Dad for one reason or another. Katie and Sophie, meanwhile, were out on the streets, getting into trouble. Katie had filled her ears up with tonnes of piercings; she had a full-on attitude problem now – very aggressive and confrontational. She and Sophie had bunked off from school so much, neither of them had any qualifications – they just ran around, doing their own thing. At seventeen, Katie fell pregnant, while Sophie, fifteen, was out getting high on cannabis, drink and anything else she could get her hands on.

I realised very quickly that all this had been kept from me while I was ill. And now, because it had become a habit, they still refused to open up to me, afraid that I could not cope with it mentally. It was infuriating. Mostly, I would just catch snippets of conversation, but when I asked what was going on, they all said it was nothing. It made me feel that I could not be trusted to rationalise or think like a normal person. I knew they didn't want to upset me but the upshot was that I was always on the outside.

As time passed Mum and Celine moved to England to live with my gran, who was suffering from terminal cancer. Katie by now had left home to live with her boyfriend and Sophie was at our dad's place. So now we were all separated for real and I saw them less and less. It killed me inside but I had to try to accept this was my life now and it was never going to be as before.

Instead, I tried to focus on my recovery. Food was no longer the centre of my world but I still tried to ensure I ate a healthy diet – lots of vegetables, pulses, grains, cereals, rice and yoghurt. I had missed food and all the pleasure it could bring so now I put on more weight and started experimenting with different products, trying out all the new vegetarian dishes as they hit the shelves. I bought food recipes and tried delicious pâtés, spreads and crackers.

Until now, I hadn't thought about getting a job – I was on Disability Benefit for a long time after I got out of hospital – and, to be honest, I had no idea what I might be qualified to do. Then, one night, in the pub that Dad was now running, I bumped into an old school friend of his called John. He asked me if I was working. I explained that I had just recovered from eating issues and, thankfully, he said he knew about this as Dad had already told him. I was pleased Dad had been talking to his friends about what I was going through – it wasn't a dirty little secret or something he was ashamed of. John offered me some labouring work with his daughter, Meredith, and, from the word go, I loved it. It felt so good to be building up my strength again and now I felt physically and mentally stronger. Every day, I carted heavy wheelbarrows filled with bricks on a building site and enjoyed every single minute of it.

After a few months of manual labour, John asked me if I would like to look after his baby boy, Brodie (his girlfriend, Devon, worked full-time so they needed a nanny to take care of their son). I jumped at the chance and, from the minute I met Brodie, I fell in love. He was the most adorable little boy – blond with large brown eyes and a cheeky smile; we immediately took to each other. I moved out of the rehabilitation unit and into their house as Brodie's full-time nanny.

Now Brodie and I went everywhere together. At Christmas, we would drive down to my mum's house in England if his parents were away or working. Several nights a week, I would take him to my gran's house, where he would play hide-and-seek under the dining table while she prepared him his favourite meal of mince and tatties.

On Sundays, my day off, my sister Sophie and I would go hill walking in the glens with our cousins, Marco and Peter. We would climb from 7 a.m. until about 6 p.m., then go to St Andrews for dinner. It felt so good to build up my muscles again and use my body. Best of all, I was seeing the world, reconnecting with nature, learning to appreciate everything that life has to offer. It wasn't just about getting fit and strong, it was about truly opening my eyes to the magic around me; I was alive and determined to make the most of it!

The mountains and hills in Scotland are dramatic, beautiful and constantly changing, thanks to the unpredictable weather. I loved making the hard climb to the top of Munro in the Highlands – reaching the summit filled me with elation. Once there, we sat side by side, just soaking up the natural beauty of the landscape, enjoying the serenity. Looking down the magnificent valley, away from the hustle and bustle of the town, I felt calm. I had been cooped up in a sterile hospital ward for too long – now I needed to see the world, to breathe it in, let it soak into my skin.

Every climb brought fresh smells, new, intoxicating sights and a firm appreciation of all that I'd missed during the past four years. The flowers, animals, birds, waterfalls and streams all took my breath away. Often, we sat at the side of a waterfall, watching how the glacial waters tumbled over the shiny pebbles and, when our feet ached, we'd peel off our socks and jump into the cool, refreshing streams.

There was one particular place I loved to climb the most: Loch Brandy. It wasn't the highest hill to climb, but to me it was definitely the most beautiful. The small loch up the hill is stone cold, but calm and ethereal. It draws you up to see her beauty and demands you give her the respect she craves. Occasionally, I asked my dad or Auntie Annette to join me on my walk there so I could share this special place with people I loved.

We would usually climb a few thousand feet and then, after an hour or so relaxing at the top, taking in the breath-taking magnificence, run all the way back down again. It was often easier than trying to walk and much more fun and exhilarating.

Celine now came up to visit us and it was lovely to share time with her. She told me that Mum was much more settled in England and, in fact, she'd met a man who seemed to make her happy. Dad, too, had moved on and, for the first time in ages, I could see we were building the foundations of a strong relationship. Day by day, my confidence was returning and the person I'd lost so many years ago was coming back to life.

Chapter 16

Reach for
the Sky

An almighty roar filled my ears as the Harrier Jump Jet engines started up and I was momentarily stunned. I had never heard anything like it in my life.

'What do you think?' my gran yelled at me over the colossal sound. She was shouting at the top of her voice but still her words were drowned out by the fearsome noise of the engine. I watched in fascination as the powerful machine lifted straight off the ground in a vertical take-off, a manoeuvre that seemed almost impossible for such a mighty craft.

'WOW!' was the only word I could get out. I was awestruck by the incredible jets, planes and helicopters all around. Gran had taken Brodie and me to the Navy Day at Rosyth Royal Dockyard in October 1991 and, from the moment I caught sight of the amazing aircraft, I was awestruck. As soon as the whine and whoosh of an engine started up, I could feel my heart begin to race, and then watching them lift off the ground to perform their aerobatic stunts was just thrilling. I couldn't believe I'd never seen a plane up close like this before and I knew then and there I had found my vocation: I wanted to be a pilot.

At twenty-two years old, I'd been looking after Brodie for nearly two years and life was settling down quite comfortably but, until that day, I had never felt a passion to achieve something. Now I was driven by a burning desire. The following Monday, I walked into the RAF careers office and told the middle-aged man behind the desk that I wanted to train to become a pilot. I might as well have told him I wanted to be a lion tamer.

'Oh-kay,' he said slowly. 'Do you have maths or higher maths qualifications?'

I shook my head.

'Do you have physics? Do you have higher chemistry?'

'No,' I replied.

'How old are you?'

'I'm twenty-two,' I replied, now bristling at this hostile interrogation.

'I'm afraid you've got no chance, lassie,' he said and smiled condescendingly. 'And you being female – well, that won't help the situation either. We've got guys coming in here – seventeen, eighteen years old – with all the right qualifications and even they struggle to get on the course.'

Then he chuckled and shook his head, as if my dream of becoming a pilot had been the joke that made his day.

I should have been mortified and left the office with my head down but, no, from somewhere deep inside, I found the confidence to tell this patronising man: 'Well, you may not want to train me but I will be a pilot one day. And it's a damn shame the RAF don't do more to encourage women to join!' And with that, I marched out.

For the first time, I had an ambition and I was not going to take no for an answer. Somehow, I was going to fly planes. I had no idea how, when or where, I just knew it was going to happen. Back at home that evening, I started researching how to become a commercial pilot. And with Dad's help, I got a loan to start training for my private pilot's licence (PPL). Within the month, I had begun flying lessons at Dundee Airport.

From the very moment I stepped inside a cockpit, I knew this was what I was meant to do. Up there, in the sky, released from the physical limitations of gravity, I felt free. Truly free! It was exhilarating beyond belief and yet, at the same time, so calm and serene. Soon afterwards, I joined the flying club and every day after work I'd rush down there for my lessons or to talk shop with the other trainee pilots and instructors. I threw myself into flying, heart, body and soul, and when I wasn't in the air, I was studying for my meteorology and navigation exams.

Nobody was going to tell me I couldn't do it. I knew I wanted it so badly, nothing could stand in my way. Suddenly, all that stubbornness and determination I had used to destroy my body in my teens was redirected to achieve a positive goal. And every day that I flew, I gained a little more confidence and skill.

I seized every opportunity to fly or to sit in with some of the more experienced pilots. I loved going up with the ones who were qualified to do the aerobatics or holding the satnav for night flying. My favourite was learning to recover from a spin. The first time I did it, I thought I was going to crash at high speed. I could not focus on anything as we spun towards the ground, but then the instructor showed me how to control the spin and pull it back into straight and level flight. I did it myself and was terrified but learned the technique very quickly, wresting back control from the spinning craft.

Over the next few months, I took my meteorology exams and, though I failed on my first two attempts, I passed third time. Navigation wasn't as hard for me and I sailed through this exam. There were a few others too that I passed without a problem. The most challenging element was landings but I pushed myself harder than anybody else and, over time, I came to learn how to bring the plane in at just the right altitude – not too high, not too low.

Finally, in the spring of 1992, my examiner passed me to go out on my own – my first solo flight. It was a huge day for me – so nerve-wracking but, at the same time, incredibly exciting. I took off in a Cessna 152 – a two-seater training aircraft – without any problems, climbed steadily, and was happy and confident that I was in control at all times.

It was only when I had reached 1,500 feet that it suddenly hit me – I was on my own! Now I had to land the plane with no one else there and, for a brief second, my confidence waivered. *Oh, God, what if I crash? What if I forget some of the crucial checks?* At that moment, I heard a little voice inside: *You can do this, Tina! You can do it. Just sit tight, relax and remember you've come back from the brink of death. You've beaten anorexia. If you can do that, you can do anything!*

All those hours in therapy learning positive reinforcement now gave me the courage I needed at this crucial moment in my life. *Yes*, I said to myself, *you CAN do this. You KNOW you can!* And so, sat there, on my own, at 1,500 feet, I started singing James Brown's 'I Feel Good' at the top of my voice and did a little seat dance! To be up there, flying on my own, was exhilarating beyond belief and I felt like I was on another plane of reality. Another 20 minutes and then it was time to bring her in; now I focused hard on the job in hand.

Landings are described as controlled crashes and, it has to be said, my landing was almost a crash! I was so nervous as I brought her in, and, for a moment, I saw I was low, *very* low! Terror, excitement, panic and determination all combined in those final few seconds as I checked and rechecked all the instruments. *Keep the power high, come in low; look at the nose attitude towards the runway. Keep the power high . . .*

My brain now was completely and fully engaged with the job in hand. It was as if my mind was a laser beam, focusing sharply on all the elements of the landing. I was in the zone! The touchdown was smooth and I smiled to myself as I felt the solid ground zoom beneath me; it had been a good landing. At that moment, I heard cheers from the control tower.

'Well done, great job!' the radio controller said through my earpiece. 'Your Dad is here – he says he's very proud of you.'

I had no idea he was in the air-traffic tower watching me the whole time. It was one of the best moments of my life. I was so proud right then. I had only learned to drive a car a year before and yet here I was, flying a plane on my own! For the first time in my life, I felt I had achieved something great and I was worthy of the praise. No one could have done that for me – it was all my own work.

As I taxied in I was so excited and overwhelmed, I forgot all my checks! I heard my instructor reminding me over my earpiece and, finally, when I got out of the plane, I could hardly stand as my legs had turned to jelly. But I wanted more: this was what I wanted to do more than anything else in my life.

Now, with my newfound vocation, my confidence grew and I started working with my dad, whose pub business was doing great trade. He decided to open up a new bar in the crypt of an old church in town, which I helped to refurbish and launch. With the help of some of my friends at the flying club, I managed to get hold of some World War II spitfire pilot maps, which we used as wallpaper, and some rare photos of jets in action. Almost overnight, the bar was a success. Now I worked there when Brodie was in nursery and, during the quiet times, when I was in the office working on the admin, he sat in with me. In my spare time, I flew.

I also joined the Territorial Army, which helped build my strength, endurance and confidence. I loved going on exercise all weekend and prided myself on being the quickest person in my group at stripping and reassembling an SA80 rifle. Since I had studied navigation, I was already ahead of the pack and it wasn't long before I was awarded the honour of Top Recruit. I was highly competitive and realised all those years of trying to make myself the best anorexic in the world had been wasted – but not any longer. Now I was grabbing life with both hands and putting all my strength and resilience to good use.

In the process, I built a new and great relationship with my dad. Working together side by side, I realised how much time we had missed out on and, now, as an adult, I could appreciate all his wonderful qualities. Dad was terrific fun – he always had a joke up his sleeve and a kind word for all his customers. All those unhappy feelings from my childhood were gone, replaced by a newfound respect and love for my father and for the person he was. I forgave him all his failings because what else could I do? If I wanted to grow and become a strong individual, I had to take responsibility for my own life and not blame my problems on the past. I couldn't change what happened but I could damn well change my future!

My mum was now remarried to a wonderful man called Reg and they were very happy together. It was great to see her come alive again – to smile and laugh easily. Reg had a pigeon loft and wore a flat cap, cycled to work every day and drank pints of bitter – he was a salt-of-the-earth kind of guy and, best of all, he adored my mother. Mum became very involved in politics and retrained in order to get involved with equal-rights issues, school committees and domestic-abuse councils. A committed and tireless worker, she was a world away from the depressed woman I knew from my teens and I was so proud of her.

Over the following months, I worked hard to pass my private pilot's licence. The main part of this was the solo cross-country flight. First, my instructor took me on a 300-mile round trip cross-country and then, when he thought I was ready, it was time to do it on my own. For months, I was prevented from taking this test because I couldn't get a break in the weather. Eventually, 18 months after I started flying, I was ready to go it alone.

It was a thrilling day and one I felt more than ready for. My route took me first from Dundee to Aberdeen, which was easy enough, and, once I was within the right airspace, I was given instructions on my height and position by air-traffic to land. At this point, I started to panic. *Where is the runway? Where is the damned runway?* I couldn't see it from my position. I knew I had followed the map correctly but I couldn't get any visuals on the place where I was actually meant to land. Now my heart started to thump wildly and my hands trembled at the controls – over the radio, I heard there was a Boeing 737 full of holidaymakers in front of me, a Bond chopper carrying offshore workers behind, all trying to get home safely. And here I was, right in the middle, with no clue on how I was going to get down in one piece! My mind started to race – was I about to be responsible for a terrible mid-air collision?

In my panic, I did a few steep turns to try to get some visual on the runway while maintaining height and position. For a few seconds, my brain froze – it felt like time had stood still as I desperately searched out the ground below for the place I was meant to bring her down. I was in the queue now and didn't have any choice – I had to land. Finally, after what felt like a lifetime, I spotted the familiar line of straight twinkling lights of the runway a few miles in front of me. *Thank God!* I could have cried with happiness at that moment but I couldn't let my emotions take over; I had to bring the plane in safely.

Oh, Christ! I knew at the moment of impact I had brought her in too hard. The plane hit the runway with a terrible thud and then went into a Pilot Induced Oscillation (PIO). It was every pilot's nightmare. The plane bounces on every wheel one at a time like a steel ball in a pinball machine, rebounding wildly from one bumper to the next. My mouth clamped down hard as I got thrown and banged about. It felt like it went on for ever but, eventually, I managed to get the plane under control and taxied into the club. Amazingly, the air-traffic controllers told me my landing looked great and sent me on my way, to find Scone in Perth Aerodrome next.

Needless to say, I was in no rush to get back up into the air. However, I didn't have a choice, so off I went. Landing this time around turned out to be a much better experience, there being no one else in the airspace when I couldn't find the notoriously difficult sloping grass runway. In fact, it was just the tonic I needed from my bruising landing in Aberdeen. Up there now, flying around and enjoying the amazing views, I was filled with a sense of calm. The landing was still a touch heavy but a million times better than Aberdeen. Finally, I headed back to Dundee – the total trip had only taken five hours and yet, in that time, I had learned so much. Landing at Dundee now seemed so easy.

Two weeks later, my private pilot's licence arrived in the post – I was so proud when I opened the envelope and saw the big brown leather book, which resembled a large passport, with my name inside. I had achieved something I never thought possible. The first thing I did was to train on another type of aircraft – a Warrior four-seater – so I could take up more passengers. My first passengers were my good friends, Shirley and Doug – they were regulars in the pub and were always really supportive of me. In fact, they'd come out with me in the car when I'd first passed my test, so I wanted them to be my first passengers in the air, too. I flew them all around Dundee and they loved it. I was so proud of myself. It was the most amazing feeling, having passengers who trusted me to take them up into the air and back down safely!

That same month, I saw an advertisement for a brand-new course in Aviation and Avionics at Dundee Airport. And so I applied. It had never been held before and all the lengthy in-depth interviews were held at Perth Aerodrome. This was my chance to get my Commercial Pilot's Licence (CPL). I was the only female to be accepted onto the course but, after a month of intense excitement, it was dropped due to lack of sponsorship by airlines. I was devastated but my determination was undimmed.

Now I applied for courses all over the world and had one earmarked at Kansas State University. I got in touch and we connected well. My fees were agreed and I was set to leave just over a year later – in January 1995. I was sad to be leaving my dad, of course, and the bar and all my friends and family, but I had a burning desire to do this and nothing was going to deter me. In the meantime, I carried on with my life at full tilt – working the bar, flying, hill walking and the TA. I had no time for anything else and I was certainly not interested in having a relationship. I was just too darn busy! And yet, on Christmas Day 1993, all that changed . . .

Chapter 17

Jock

Christmas Day 1993 – the bar was fizzing with joy as I rushed around in my pinstripe trousers and white shirt, taking orders, serving drinks and greeting all our customers. Christmas was always the best time to work in Dad's bar – we had a great kitchen and prided ourselves on serving good food, so it was little wonder we were usually full and mad busy. There was a buzz and hum to the restaurant that day as families toasted each other, pulled crackers and weaved tipsily through the tables to wish each other a 'Happy Christmas'.

By 1 p.m., service was in full swing and there were only a couple of tables yet to arrive. Just then, Ally and George, two of our regulars, came down the stairs into the dining room from the pub above, ready to take their places for lunch. I looked up briefly, checking them off against the reservations list in our book and, at that moment, I got the shock of my life. Following them down the stairs was a very tall, handsome man with dark hair and eyes. I couldn't look away – he was gorgeous! I don't know what happened to me then but it was like I was struck by a feeling I'd never experienced before. I couldn't take my eyes off him for a second! Eventually, I pulled myself together enough to grab three menus and waded through the tables to greet my friends.

'Ally! George! Merry Christmas!'

'Merry Christmas, Tina!' they both replied, and smiled back at me.

'And who's your friend here?' I asked straight away, keeping my eyes locked on his. I saw then that he was grinning broadly and I couldn't help smiling back.

'Tina, meet Jock.' I put my hand out and he took mine in a strong, firm grip. I didn't hesitate for a second. It was as if an invisible force was drawing me towards him. Wow, this was something else! All of a sudden, it felt like the room was spinning and I could see from the look in his eye that he knew. He *knew*! But I had to get down to business, so I showed them to their table and went back to the bar to get their drinks order. Oh, my God, I could hardly think straight! What was happening to me? I was dizzy; I was in love! I kept stealing glances at Jock, and every time I did so, I found he was staring straight back at me; it was electric. My heart thumped crazily in my chest and my legs went to jelly.

'Here, Janine!' I caught one of the waitresses on her way back to the bar with an empty tray. 'Can you take these drinks to table four, please?' I nodded over at Ally's table.

'Aye, no problem!' she replied, not even questioning why

I couldn't do it myself. I wanted to – very badly – I wanted any excuse to get back to that man again but, the fact was, I was shaking so much, I was afraid I would spill their drinks. I wanted to know Jock, I *had* to know Jock; I knew in my heart I was in love.

The rest of the lunch service passed in a complete blur – we were so busy, I hardly had time to think and yet all I wanted to do was go over and speak to Jock. But what could I say? Though I had dated a couple of guys in the last few years, there had been nothing serious and I had never in my life felt so strongly before. My head and heart were all over the place. It was hard enough to keep focused on the customers.

Eventually, and without my noticing, the clock rolled around to 4 p.m. and, before I knew it, I was staring at an empty dining room. They had left half an hour before and I was so busy, I hadn't even got to say goodbye! Now, as the final customers moved up to the pub, I sank down onto a stool. What if I never saw him again? Had I blown this one chance? After all the adrenalin and excitement of the afternoon, I felt drained and mystified. *What happened today?* It just didn't make any sense.

The next few days dragged by as my thoughts tumbled round my head. I couldn't get this man out of my mind and yet he was a complete stranger to me. It was such a relief when Ally came in a few days later – I was all prepared to interrogate her when she opened with: 'Hey, Tina – Jock has been asking about you!'

My heart nearly exploded with happiness. He had asked about *me*! He liked me, too!

'Yeah?' I was grinning like an idiot. 'And what did you say?'

'I said: "You've got no chance with Tina, Jock. She's only interested in flying, the Army, hill climbing and reading!"'

This was annoying – it was true I wasn't flirtatious and had never shown the slightest bit of interest in most men, but this was different.

'So what did he say to that?' I was trying to be casual.

'He just smiled! I told him, though – I said he's too old for you! He's thirty-five.'

'Really? I thought he was very good-looking, actually.'

Ally's eyes widened with surprise.

'Are you joking? We've all got a sweepstake that you would be the last person in the world to get into a serious relationship!'

'Cheeky buggers!' I laughed. 'Well, you never know! Tell me about him.'

'Aye, well, he's a lovely guy, I'll tell you that. Sad story, though – he's got two boys from his marriage, which broke up just over a year ago. He caught her having an affair – with his friend and everything. Poor man! Anyway, he sees his boys at the weekend. That's why he was with us on Christmas Day – the bairns were with their mum.

'He was a well-known ice-hockey player in his day and he's still involved with coaching, but he moved into the oil industry and now he's an electrician.'

I was more intrigued than ever. That evening, as I was mulling over this information, Dad came over to the bar stool where I was sitting.

'A penny for them?' he asked.

'What?'

'A penny for your thoughts – what's up?'

'Oh, nothing.'

Dad's eyebrows shot up — he clearly wasn't about to be fobbed off.

'All right, then.' I was close to my dad now and I didn't see why I couldn't share this with him. 'It's that bloke, Jock — you know, the one who came in with Ally and George on Christmas Day?'

'Aye.'

'Well, he seems like a really nice guy and, I suppose, I was thinking about him. You know?'

Dad breathed in deeply and looked at me with a funny, lopsided smile. He knew *exactly* what I meant!

'Jock, eh? Do you ken how auld he is?' Dad asked. 'And he has two bairns!'

'Aye, I know that.' I smiled at Dad then. I heard in those words the protective father in him speaking — he didn't want me to get hurt. But I was a grown woman now and could make my own mind up.

'I know that, Dad, and it doesn't matter. Not to me, anyway.'

The truth was, I was dying to see Jock again — I just didn't know how that was going to happen. Luckily for me, I didn't have to figure it out.

Occasionally, I worked in the bar owned by Brodie's parents and a couple of weeks after Christmas, while I was doing their books, Jock wandered in. I was shocked to see him there but delighted and very nervous. He'd not been off my mind the whole time. As soon as we looked at each other, a bolt of electricity went coursing through my body. My stomach flipped over and I broke into a wide smile. He beamed back — God, he was gorgeous!

We exchanged 'hello's' and made some small talk about Christmas and Ally and George. He asked me what I had been up to the past few weeks and, for a second, my mind went blank. *Does he know? Can he tell I'm a bundle of nerves?* It took all the will I had not to reply: *Thinking about you!* I told him about my flying and how I was learning to do aerobatics. He seemed really interested and we would have chatted longer but I had work to be getting on with and John was behind the bar, watching me. So I said a hurried goodbye and went to the back office. I thought I'd blown it again but, a week later, Jock was back in my dad's bar and again we fell to talking.

Finally, after four of these supposedly coincidental meetings, Jock asked me out to see a film with him. I wanted to scream but I just replied, 'Sure.' It turned out that I had to take Brodie that evening but I didn't think this was a bad thing. After all, Brodie was a huge part of my life and I knew that if he liked someone, it would be okay. So we all went to see a comedy movie together and had a ball. Brodie loved Jock straight away and Jock was really good with him – very funny and sweet. We giggled the whole way through the film. It was a perfect first date – extremely relaxed and fun. On my way home that night, I thought: *I'm going to marry this man!*

The next week, we met alone and this time went for a drive. As we sat in the car, looking out onto the beach at Broughty Ferry, Jock opened up to me about his children and family situation. He explained that he had discovered his wife of seven years having an affair with his friend and boss at the gym. Jock had been an ice-hockey player and his wife, Dawn, had been a figure skater; they met at the ice rink and fell in love and had two boys, Steven and Danny, together. He had left the marital home the year before and moved in with his mum and dad. Now he was working as an electrician and saw his boys every weekend.

I could see he wanted to be straight with me from the start and I loved that about him. There was no playing games – we both felt strongly from the word go and the way he talked was so sincere. It was clear he adored his boys and though it had obviously been a very difficult situation, he had come to terms with the breakdown of his marriage; he was ready to move on. I tried to let him know that I was fine with it, too – it didn't put me off in the least.

After that, Jock and I started seeing each other all the time – we connected in so many ways. I knew we were both deeply in love but he was such a gentleman that he didn't want to rush the physical side of things. In fact, it wasn't until months after our first date that I kissed him! I was so desperate that I just gave him a peck on the cheek and I suppose that started the ball rolling.

A few weeks later, I opened up about my past. I told Jock everything about being anorexic, nearly dying, spending my teens in a psychiatric ward and how it had taken me years to recover. It was hard – I had never really talked to anyone about this and I felt deeply ashamed of myself but he had to know! He had been so honest with me and I didn't want to hide anything either. Nevertheless, it was a nerve-wracking evening when it all came pouring out. I was afraid he would think I was unbalanced and unsuitable for a long-term relationship. But Jock took it all in his stride – he listened really carefully to everything and then afterwards, he said: 'You've done so well, Tina. You should be proud of yourself.' Then he pulled me into him for an enormous bear hug. It was the best reaction I could have hoped for!

When the time came, the physical side of our relationship was easy, so natural and loving. I didn't have any body hang-ups now and felt so comfortable with Jock. He was a devoted boyfriend. Whenever I had a TA exercise weekend, he'd collect me from the barracks, cook me a lovely meal and then drive me back home so I could get to bed for work on Monday morning. Brodie loved him and we started going out with his boys, as well as my nieces when they were free. I was always careful to give Jock as much alone time with his sons as possible but, at the same time, I loved meeting up with them – they were such good kids. Danny was only two and Steven was seven. We all went ice-skating at the weekends and Jock taught them all to ice-skate. Often, we joined Jock at ice-hockey games, too.

In September 1994, Jock bought me a Breitling watch in my favourite colour of racing green. It was the watch that every pilot wanted and he said it was for when I left for Kansas to start training as a commercial pilot. It was beautiful and I loved it so much but, most of all, I loved Jock. I told him there and then I could never leave him. It was true – I'd been thinking about Kansas for some time and, despite all my dreams, I had found love and I wasn't about to throw that away for anything in the world. I would have to find another way of becoming a pilot.

'Are you sure?' Jock asked me for the millionth time in bed that night.

'Yes, I'm certain, Jock,' I whispered into the darkness. 'I won't leave you. Don't worry – I'll never stop flying. I'll just have to find another way.'

Two weeks later, I was working in the bar when I was suddenly overcome with nausea and had to sit down. Dad asked me if I was okay.

'I don't know, Dad,' I said, squinting up towards him, my hand on my head. 'I haven't been feeling all that good recently. I'm just really tired all the time.'

'Aye, well, you're looking a little peaky now. Why don't you get yourself down the doctor's this afternoon?'

So that's what I did. And when the doctor asked me if I thought I could be pregnant, I just scoffed: 'No way! I'm on the Pill.'

'Aye, well, better to be certain one way or the other. We'll do a pregnancy test, anyway.'

I got the shock of my life when it turned out positive! A baby! I was too young to have children. Jock and I had only been seeing each other for seven months – we had no house together, we weren't even engaged. I was living in Brodie's parents' place still. This was crazy!

I was still in a daze when Jock picked me up 20 minutes later, but I didn't waste any time. As soon as I got into the car in the car park, I broke the news.

Jock was as shocked as me: 'Really? I thought you were on the Pill.'

'I am, I don't know how it's happened but I'm pregnant.'

There was a silence then and Jock let his hands drop from the steering wheel as he tried to get his head around this strange turn of events.

'How do you feel about it?' he asked me.

'I'm shocked but, well, I suppose, we'll just have to make this work.'

He didn't miss a beat: 'That's right, whatever you want. We love each other so we can make this work.'

As the weeks passed, I felt more and more excited. We decided not to tell anybody until after our 12-week scan but, secretly, I was so pleased. This could be the start of a proper family for myself – something I had always wanted. All those years without a period had left a niggling uncertainty in the back of my mind: *What if I couldn't conceive? What if I'd destroyed my own fertility?* Now I knew that I was able to have children and it was so lovely that I was about to fulfil my dreams of motherhood with the love of my life.

It was mid-December 1994 and I was cleaning up the bar after a huge Christmas party the night before when, suddenly, I felt a gushing down below, then my knickers were soaked. I rushed to the toilets and, there, I saw I was bleeding heavily. After seeing a doctor, I was immediately sent to hospital, where a scan confirmed my worst fears – I was miscarrying the baby.

It was devastating – I went home that night and cried into Jock's arms. I was booked into hospital the next day for a DNC – a formal procedure to scrape out the lining of the uterus. Of course, it was horrible and I hated every minute. Afterwards, I felt so empty and alone. That special, secret feeling I'd been carrying around inside me was gone and in its place was desolation and despair. I had imagined our baby and our new life together – I had seen myself cradling it and felt the certainty of the bond we would share. Now all that was shattered and I was distraught.

Jock tried to reassure me as best he could. It wasn't meant to be, he said. It was Nature's way of telling us there was something wrong with the pregnancy. He held me and stroked my hair but, in the early hours of the morning, I mourned for the little life I'd carried for such a very short time.

Nevertheless, I had no choice. I had to pick myself up and move on. Nobody had known about the pregnancy, so I couldn't grieve publicly – I just tried to focus on the positives in our lives and get through the days without weeping.

Then, just three weeks later, I was working at the bar as usual, when I got a frenzied phone call from Jock. His words froze my soul.

'Tina, something terrible has happened,' he said. 'We need to talk. This could really affect our future together.'

I wasted no time – I told the bar staff I had to leave and jumped in the car. At his parents' house, I was met by a shaky and red-eyed Jock, who took me through to the kitchen to break the news. The boys were with his mum in the living room.

'It's Dawn,' he started. 'She's left the country and abandoned the boys.'

'*What?*' I could hardly believe what he was saying.

'It's true! She took the boys to the Hilton Hotel over Christmas. While they were there, Dawn and her boyfriend arranged for all their furniture and personal belongings to be shipped abroad. We knew nothing until they dropped the boys off at my mum's house, two hours ago. Everything was normal and then about ten minutes later, Mum got a call from Dawn, asking if they were still at home. Mum said yes, and within fifteen minutes there was a taxi at the door with two brown envelopes, one for me and one for my folks. They were letters explaining that they had left the country. In the envelope were the benefits book and the keys to the house so we could collect the boys' stuff. That's it! They've sold the house and gone.'

It was too much – I could barely take in the enormity of what he was saying.

'She's left? Just like that?'

'It wasn't a spur-of-the-moment thing, Tina. They've been planning this for months! In the letter she wrote to me, she said she won't be pursuing visitation rights as her life is with her boyfriend now and not with the children.'

I could hardly believe a mother would do something like that to her own children. It beggared belief.

Jock's eyes filled with tears and I could hear the terrible anguish in his voice as he whispered: 'How could she do this to our children? What am I going to say to them?'

I felt so bad for him then but I knew one thing for certain: 'I'll help you. I'll be right by your side,' I told him firmly. 'This doesn't change anything between us. I love you and we'll get through this together. I'm not going anywhere – I promise.'

We hugged then and, after talking things through, we decided to fetch the boys' things from the house. It was eerie. Their beds were still made with all their teddies neatly lined up. The drawers were stacked with their clean clothes and yet the rest of the house was full of rubbish Dawn and her boyfriend did not want. The only furniture that remained was a leather sofa and a table; the rest had been cleared out.

We went back to Jock's parents' house, where the boys were

with his mum, playing, still blissfully unaware of the dramatic events of the last few hours.

He called them into the living room and we sat them down together. Jock chose his words carefully: 'Boys, I'm really sorry to have to tell you this but your mum has gone and I don't know when she's going to be back again.'

Steven, now eight years old, was thunderstruck. He started to cry uncontrollably, the way only a child can cry – big, heaving, snotty, gulping sobs. It broke my heart. Jock locked him into a bear hug and they stayed like that a while, until Steven had breath enough to say: 'She didn't say goodbye to us! Why didn't she say goodbye?'

We had no answers for him. At three years old, Danny didn't really understand what was going on but the way everyone was so upset made him cry and Jock grabbed him, too. The three of them stayed like that for a while – Jock's face obscured, buried into the heads of his now motherless sons.

I was so very sad for these children. It was a completely different life for them now. They would live with Jock at his parents' place until he found somewhere of his own.

That night, after we put the children to bed, Jock sat me down. He looked troubled and I could see there was something on his mind.

'Look, Tina,' he started. 'I know what you said before but I want you to think about this seriously now. I would understand if you wanted to stop seeing me. I mean, this situation, it's . . . I'm a single dad with two boys to raise on my own. I don't want—'

I didn't let him get any further.

'You're *not* a single dad,' I said vehemently. 'You have me and we're doing this together. There's no question in my mind that the boys are part of my future and I love you way too much to let anything tear us apart. You're not on your own – we'll make this work together.'

So that was that. We were going to make it work, come what may. I couldn't imagine what had led Dawn to abandon her children in this way – it was so cold and calculating – but I wasn't about to walk out of their lives, too. It brought fresh tears to my eyes just thinking about it.

Steven confided in me that night, saying his mother hadn't even hugged him goodbye that morning. She knew this was the last time she would see her son and yet, she couldn't even give him a hug. What sort of mother does that? No, these children needed love and stability more than ever before, and Jock needed to be supported in getting through this. I would help them all, I decided. I wouldn't let them down.

Chapter 18

Breakdown

*K*ilkenny. *Kilkenny. Kilkenny. Kilkenny . . . Why? Why is this word going round and round in my head?*

I stacked the dirty glasses neatly in the dishwasher under the bar, being careful not to let them clink against one another, but still this name of an Irish beer would not go away. *Kilkenny. Kilkenny. Kilkenny . . .* As I bent down under the bar, I whispered the word to myself: 'Kilkenny.' If I said it, maybe it would go away – but it didn't. Real voices now shouted for my attention.

'When you're ready, Tina?'

'Pint of Guinness please, love!'

'Tina, are you serving or what?'

I tried to stack faster as I shouted over to the waiting customers: 'Give us a moment, lads!'

But now that strange tightening sensation around my head had started up, like someone had wrapped a band around my forehead and was pulling tightly on it. It wasn't the first time. This bizarre feeling was happening more and more frequently. I looked up and blinked – the lights in the bar were far too bright. They almost blinded me! It was March 1995 now and, for the last few weeks, I had started to feel very odd and anxious all the time, as if my adrenalin was soaring. In that heightened state of fear, I found I could not eat. It wasn't the anorexia – I was into good habits now and had maintained a normal weight of 9 stone for years. No, this was entirely physical. My stomach was constantly turning over with fear. *Don't be so stupid, Tina*, I scolded myself over and over. *You've got no reason to be anxious!*

But still the feeling wouldn't leave and, as I started to lose weight, I noticed this tightening around my head, as if my skin was shrinking. Lights became an issue. It was too bright everywhere I went. I had to shield my eyes just to get out of the house in the morning. And random words began to haunt me. Today, the word was 'Kilkenny'. I knew it was the name of one of our beers but I couldn't stop it from marching round my head, pulsating in my brain like a metronome. The word filled my mind and stopped me from hearing the interactions in the bar. Nothing I did could get rid of it. I was also very aware that my eyes felt as if they were staring madly, and when I spoke my voice sounded like I had a tin pot on my head. I became scared to speak or look at people in case they noticed it or become scared.

What's happening to you, Tina? I asked myself over and over again. Every day, I woke up, hoping these strange feelings would have left overnight, but they just got worse over the next three weeks. My confidence took a rapid dive and it got to the point where I didn't want to be alone. I never told a soul what was going through my head in case they thought I was going mad and locked me up. But all my fears from the years on the ward came flooding back and I recalled the people I had met there, with all their different illnesses. My mind summoned up Lorraine and the big black shape she had seen in the road, swallowing people up. *Was that happening to me now? No!* I refused to let the thought get any further – I was so terrified and ashamed at the idea of losing my mind, I just tried to ignore the butterflies that constantly lived in my stomach. Every day, I told myself to carry on and forget it, but I was still living my life at breakneck speed and now I had Jock's boys to look after, too.

My sister now Sophie lived on the top floor of a beautiful old building and, on the first Saturday in April, I went to see her. It was a beautiful spring day and, as usual, the sun shone so brightly, I had to wear sunglasses. I climbed the giant stone staircase up to the fifth floor of the building to her flat, where Sophie let me in with a great big hug. We'd grown so close recently and it was always lovely to see her. She sat me down with a cup of tea but, within a few minutes, I was overcome by a powerful, almost magnetic urge to run and jump out of the window. I planted my feet firmly on the floor, trying to root myself to the wooden floorboards to stop the force, but now there was a voice in my head that kept repeating the word: *JUMP*. I struggled to resist the voice but, with every second that passed, it was becoming louder and more urgent: *JUMP. JUMP. JUMP. JUMP.*

My hand gripped the arms of the chair – I was terrified.

'Hey, Tina – are you all right?' Sophie's eyes creased with concern. But I couldn't answer; I was too frightened to allow my concentration to drop in case I ran to the window. I had to fight the force inside me, which was so overwhelming I couldn't let go of the chair. *Why? Why was it doing this to me?* I didn't want to die. Still, the voice inside kept making me turn back to the huge bay windows that looked out over the River Tay. *Just run and get it over with. NOW! JUMP!*

At that point, I knew I was fighting for my life and, whatever happened, I had to leave the room safely. I stood up and, as I did so, I could feel part of me pulling my body towards the window. It felt like an invisible rope was around my torso, tugging me and pulling my legs. *No! No, I don't want to do it!* I yelled inside my head. Then I turned and ran out of the flat and down all the flights of stairs. I was so determined to get down, I fell and stumbled, landing on my bottom and back a few times, but I didn't care and hardly felt the bumps – I had to get to the bottom before the voice took over.

Somewhere up above my head, I could hear desperate shouts from my sister: 'Tina? *TINA!* WHERE ARE YOU GOING? WHAT'S WRONG?'

But I couldn't stop for a second – this was a matter of life and death. Once safely on the street, I jumped straight in my car, tears now coursing down my cheeks, and turned my key in the ignition. There was no time to waste. I knew I was losing my mind and I had to get help fast, before I hurt myself. I drove home and threw some clothes in black bin bags. Brodie's mother was in the house and he was playing football across the road at his friend's. I was meant to be looking after him later that day.

'I'm sorry,' I garbled to his mum, Devon, when she came to the door. 'I can't take Brodie today, I've got to leave. Something's happened and I need help.'

'*What?* What are you talking about?' Devon replied, both cross and surprised.

'I've got to go, I'm sorry,' I repeated.

'Come on, Tina!' she barked. 'Pull yourself together. There's nothing wrong with you. Just give yourself a shake now. Your face is all squint — what a mess!'

It was too much — she had no idea of the gravity of the situation and I couldn't cope with her anger. I mumbled 'sorry' then dashed to my car, her angry shouts still ringing in my ears: 'How can you do this to us, Tina? Why are you abandoning Brodie like this?'

It was horrifying and I couldn't believe that, after being 'normal' for so long, this was happening. I needed help and I could not stay there another minute. It broke my heart. I loved that boy more than life itself but I needed to get myself sorted out.

I drove straight to Liff Hospital, as I didn't know whether the units at Ninewells were there any more. I ran straight into the unit, bags in hand, and started shouting: 'Please help me! Can someone please help?'

A few nurses came rushing forward — they could see I was in distress.

'Please,' I started to cry. 'I've been under Dr Ballinger for years but I think I'm actually going mad. My name is Tina Halford and I need some help.' I was desperate to tell them who I was and my history before I lost it completely. I had never experienced anything like this before and didn't know how long I had before my mind went completely. A smell filled my nostrils — it was a dark, foreboding smell, as if something very bad was about to happen. I tried desperately to cling onto the real world, to make sense of the thoughts in my brain and force the words out in the right order. It wouldn't be long now ...

'It's okay, Tina,' said a nurse gently as she took my arm. 'It's okay, just calm down. Take your time, we'll get a doctor to come and see you.'

They led me into a side room with a big table, and the relief at being in a place of safety where I knew I couldn't hurt myself was overwhelming.

'I need to tell my dad,' I said to a nurse. 'I need to let him know where I am.'

It was a race against time – someone had to know where I was before I lost it completely. My dad was called and, in the next few minutes, I was assessed, given some tablets and taken to bed. As I was led to the bed, the walls of the ward faded in and out, and the people around me became blurry and distant. I sensed a scream bubble up from deep inside and, in that moment, it felt like I was falling, falling backwards into a dark hole, and I was powerless to stop it. I couldn't hold it back any longer. Down I went, down, down, down ...

Chapter 19

Hospital Again

'. . . my mum with these pillows. These pillow here.'

I fought my way through the fug of sleep to hear a voice from somewhere overhead. The voice belonged to a woman and, slowly, very slowly, I managed to prise my eyes open, despite sticky, uncooperative eyelids.

Where am I?

For a moment, I had no recollection of coming to hospital, so I couldn't work out why I was in bed on a ward.

A very strange-looking woman was standing over me, staring at a point just above my head. She was a large, middle-aged lady in a nightdress, with short, wiry hair cut erratically, wearing tartan slippers on the wrong feet. She seemed fixated by something behind my head and nodded, as if I had just spoken, confirming her point of view.

'Yes,' she repeated. 'It was these pillows.'

'*What?*' I asked, still very dazed and groggy.

'These pillow here, yes,' she said, nodding again, more emphatically this time, her pale grey eyes boring into me. 'These pillows were used to suffocate my mum; these ones here.'

'Oh, right,' I said, and nodded back; to which the woman, as if sensing I had finally got the message, shuffled away to another bed, and I breathed out a long sigh. Now I knew – I was back on a psychiatric ward after nearly five years! Immediately, I recalled the terrible events that had led up to this: I remembered the feeling of being dragged towards the windows in my sister's flat, the certain knowledge that I needed help or I would kill myself. I looked around and sighed again – it was depressing to be back on a ward. I'd forgotten what a strange world this was, how the people and the place moved to its own rhythms and rules. Like Pillow Lady, I felt disconnected from reality, cut off from the rational world, unable to make it fit with my own internal logic. Something had gone very badly wrong and I still had no idea what it was.

I leaned back gingerly on my arms, pushed myself up to a sitting position and then swung my legs over the side. How long had I been asleep for? I felt very odd and woozy but, at the same time, there was a familiar pressure on my bladder and I knew I couldn't delay a visit to the loo for much longer. My bones seemed to crunch in revolt as I eased myself down onto my feet; my whole body was stiff as a board. Just then, a nurse came past and her eyes widened with surprise when she saw me.

'Ah, Miss Halford!' She smiled, looking very pleased to see me. 'You're awake! How are you?'

'Okay, I think,' I replied, rubbing my forehead, to chase away the last remnants of sleep. 'I'm not really sure. What's going on? How long have I been here for?'

'You've been asleep a very long time, Miss Halford,' she replied. 'Two days! Your dad and boyfriend have both been in several times to check on you and they're coming back later today.'

Jock! My heart at once soared and crumbled. What would he think of me now? I was terrified he wouldn't want to be with me any more. And who could blame him? I might never recover my senses – or I could be in and out of hospital for the rest of my life. I still had no idea what was happening to me – all I knew was that I felt emotionally and psychologically drained. I was empty, sad and very, very frightened.

'What's wrong with me?' I asked the nurse, suddenly gripped with impatience. 'Have I gone mad?'

'*Noooo!*' The nurse smiled indulgently. 'Don't be daft! You just need to rest and now that you're awake, the doctor will come and see you. Don't worry, Tina – everything's going to be okay.'

I smiled and asked if I could have a cigarette – she gave me one of her own and took me to the smoking room. She held a lighter at one end, while I greedily sucked at the other. But it had been two days since I'd last smoked and the powerful nicotine hit made my head spin so much, I thought I was going to pass out.

'Careful now!' the kind nurse said, laughing, as she grabbed at my arm. 'We don't want to lose you!'

Twenty minutes later, a doctor came round, to tell me that I was to be transferred to Ninewells for my treatment, since it was an environment I was used to. Then I was taken by ambulance to the old psychiatric ward where I had spent most of my teenage years, the place I used to call my second home. Only this time, I didn't want to go; of course I didn't – it felt like I was taking a massive step backwards. But at the same time, I couldn't prevent the horrible thoughts from crowding my mind any longer. It was too much – terrifying scenarios played out in my head almost constantly now and I was gripped by an intense fear I couldn't shift. It was like living in a waking nightmare. If I had to get help, if I had to be incarcerated, this was probably the best place for me.

The unit was unchanged – almost exactly as it had been years before – yet *I* was different. I didn't feel like I fitted in here now; I was an outsider. Just like many of the people I'd met years before, my mind was suddenly being ripped apart and I didn't know what the hell was going on. I was lost, confused and scared. I didn't even recognise any of the patients or nurses – I felt so out of place but, also, out of time. It was like being taken back to your old primary school as an adult and asked to fit in. Uncomfortable and unsettled, I waited to see somebody I recognised.

Eventually, my spirits rose when Dr Ballinger came to see me. She was just like before – small, kind, ruddy-cheeked and full of life. I was worried she would be disappointed with me but she didn't betray any emotions like that. If anything, she appeared very happy to see me. We chatted for a while about my symptoms and everything that had been happening in my life.

'What's wrong with me?' I asked her after a while. 'Is it to do with the contraceptive injection, a chemical imbalance?'

I was determined to find a physical cause of my mental breakdown, frightened to admit that my mind had snapped of its own accord.

'No, it's nothing to do with that,' Dr Ballinger said. 'You are suffering from psychosis brought on by anxiety. It appears you've gone through a hell of a lot recently – what with losing the baby and your partner's wife leaving the country. This stress and uncertainty has created a heightened state of agitation. What you describe as light sensitivity is due to the fact that you have dilated pupils. This is because your body is flooded with adrenalin since you are constantly in "fight or flight" mode. That's why you've been unable to eat or relax. Your body hasn't rested in a long time and now you need to take some time here to relax so we can treat you for this. Okay, Tina?'

It was such a relief to be back in Dr Ballinger's care again – I just nodded and smiled at her. In fact, right then and there, I didn't believe her – I was still convinced that I had been given a chemical imbalance from the injection. But because she had treated me successfully before, I knew I could trust her. She had cured me of anorexia and I had confidence that she could do it again. In that regard, I felt lucky – I wasn't on such unfamiliar territory that I had lost hope. No, the doctors here were good, decent and professional people. They had saved my life on so many occasions in the past, and I knew they could do the same for me this time, as long as I had faith.

The first thing they did was to start me on a course of antipsychotic drugs and I was booked in for daily psychotherapy sessions; I badly needed it. By now, my head was flooded with terrible thoughts of awful things happening to the people I loved. I was afraid that someone was out to kill me. Danger, death and despair filled my every waking moment. I didn't want to be conscious any more because my mind was full of pure horror – all the worst possible scenarios of my family and Jock and the boys dying were played out in my head over and over again in fine, gory detail. I didn't know how to stop it – I felt powerless to beat down the images and ideas, which Dr Ballinger described as 'intrusive thoughts'.

'We all have them,' she explained during one of our sessions. 'All people have them. They are unwelcome thoughts, images or ideas that just pop into our heads without warning or bidding. For example, I had an involuntary thought this morning of pushing a traffic warden off a bridge. But the difference between my involuntary thoughts and yours at this moment is that I can put them out of my mind pretty quickly. I recognise what they are and I can dismiss them. We have to work together now on giving you the tools to bring your intrusive thoughts under control.'

Dad and Jock visited every day. At first, I was worried what Jock would think of me. I mean, he'd known about the anorexia but, I guess, he assumed, like me, that it was all in the past. Now, here I was, in bed on a psychiatric ward, drugged, scared and confused.

'Here,' Jock said, smiling at me, after another one of my regular panics, and pulled me in for a hug. 'Come here, silly! I'm not going to leave you. Tina, I love you and I mean that. I'd never leave you – never, ever. I'll be with you for ever so just stop worrying about that. I'm always going to be here for you.'

He had to reassure me a lot but, eventually, his words began to sink in and his daily visits reminded me that he wasn't shrinking away from my illness. If anything, he was supporting me more than ever before. He even brought the boys in to see me, which always cheered me up so much. Dad visited most days, too, and Sophie and Katie also came. Then, I got a beautiful card from Celine, who was down in England still, and her positive, loving words brought a huge amount of comfort and encouragement. I felt surrounded by love.

At first, the doctors had to play around with my drugs to make sure they got the right type and dosage. They gave me one that made the skin on my face go numb – I felt like I was wearing a mask. Other drug combinations gave me sickness, tremors, slow movements, inability to swallow and blurred vision. It was a slow process of trial and error but, once they found the right drug, I had no unwelcome side effects. Over the next few weeks, I spent a lot of time in bed, sleeping. Being asleep was the best escape from the horrors I was having while awake.

Each day, I was woken up and taken to see the doctor, to chat for an hour. Then, I went back to sleep until lunchtime. After lunch, I had some occupational therapy to help with my concentration, which by now was completely shot. I could not focus on anything for more than a minute at a time; it meant I couldn't read or even watch TV because every plotline left me confused. It was hard not to beat myself up about my situation. I was angry that I had let myself down, that I'd failed again, but Dr Ballinger didn't let me wallow in self-pity.

'You'll never get well again until you stop being so hard on yourself,' she told me. 'Tina, your mental breakdown was a totally natural reaction to a very stressful and difficult situation. You know as well as I that this can happen to anyone at any time. It is nothing to be ashamed of, and nothing to get angry over. Just concentrate on your recovery now and the positive thoughts that will allow you to get back to your life.'

I took her words on board – in fact, I felt very lucky in many ways. I knew others who had been through this kind of experience and had attempted suicide before getting to the point of a hospital admission. Thanks to my past experiences and the people I'd met at a young age, I had recognised the signs and sought out help before it was too late.

Over the following weeks, I started to feel better and it wasn't long before the psychotherapy helped to put my situation into perspective. I realised that Dawn's unexpected departure had brought back harrowing memories from my own disrupted childhood. The unexpected absence of a parent, which suddenly threw me into a position of responsibility – I had lived through all of this before. And the feeling of being out of control, of everything overwhelming me. It was almost identical to the feelings I'd experienced as a young girl. No wonder I had reacted so strongly.

I was discharged in mid-June 1995, six weeks after being admitted to hospital. It was a relief to know that I was mentally strong enough to get back to my real life but, on the drive home, I admitted to Dad that I was nervous about returning to work.

'You've got nothing to be scared of,' he reassured me. 'They all love you and want to support you in your recovery. Don't you dare feel ashamed! You've made amazing progress and you have worked so hard to put yourself back on track. I'm proud of you, Tina. I really am!'

Still, I couldn't help it. I was shaking when I went back to the bar the next day. Would they look at me like I was a monster now? Would they treat me any differently? I tried not to let my uncertainties show when I pushed open the doors – I wanted them to see I wasn't ashamed, that I had my head high. Thankfully, everyone was so happy to see me, it was lovely. They asked how I was doing – not in that scared way I imagined they would, but with genuine care. I felt well now and the best thing was to have normal light again coming into my eyes. The intrusive thoughts were under control and I was back to eating and sleeping normally.

Still, the doctors kept a close eye on me. I attended the Outpatient's clinic once a week and my medication went on for another month. Finally, I felt back to myself again – and happy, too. In the months leading up to my breakdown, I had stopped laughing; I'd been so on edge all the time, I couldn't relax.

I went to live with Jock at his parents' and, whenever I had a day off, I would go to see Brodie. I was no longer his nanny – after all, I had been gone a long time and his parents needed to find a replacement. Moreover, I had my own family to care for now and the boys needed me at home. It was a very difficult adjustment for me – Brodie had been such a huge part of my life for the past five years and I missed him so much that I often took him out into town, to spend time with him in the park or museum. I reassured him that I still loved him no matter what and would always be there for him.

But I couldn't explain what had happened to me or why

I had left him for nearly two months; he was still too young to understand. I just hoped that by returning to his side and reassuring him, he wouldn't feel abandoned. The guilt weighed heavily on me – I cried many nights over Brodie.

'He knows how you feel,' Jock said to me one night when I got a little weepy.

'Yes, but what about when I wasn't there? God knows what he must have been thinking!' I sobbed. 'I know what it's like – kids blame themselves when you go away. They always do!'

'Maybe, but remember, you're not his mum or dad. And this is not your childhood. He'll be fine. You came back and you've told him and shown him how much you love him. You haven't disappeared – he's still a massive part of your life. You've got to stop projecting your own issues onto him. He's a very happy, loved and contented little boy – and he knows you love him dearly.'

Jock was right: my own abandonment issues were not Brodie's. I couldn't impose them onto him. Jock always knew exactly what to say to make me feel better. Far from tearing us apart, the trauma and difficulties of the past few months had only deepened and strengthened our love. He knew me better than anyone and I was confident now that nothing could come between us. We'd been to the bottom and we'd fought our way back up, as a couple, as a team; we were united.

In November that same year, the four of us – me, Jock and his two sons, Steven and Danny – moved into a small, two-bedroom bungalow near Jock's parents' and, for the first time, it felt like we were building our future together. By Christmas, we had redecorated and bought new furniture with the help of our parents, really making the house our own. Now, instead of running around at the bar on Christmas Day, Jock and I cooked an intimate family lunch for the four of us. We had to start making our own memories and it felt right that we were together on this special day, a day that was, after all, the anniversary of when we first met.

'What's this?' I asked after I came back from delivering empty plates to the kitchen after our main meal. There, on the table, in front of my seat, was a pretty green box with a crimson bow.

'Open it,' said Jock casually, picking up more plates and moving through to the kitchen. I pulled open the ribbon and eased the lid off the box. There, inside, was a black scrunchie hairband. At first, that was all I saw – *He got me a hairband for Christmas?*

Just a second later, I caught the unmistakable glint of gold – and then I saw the sparkle of the diamond. I screamed! There, in the centre of the scrunchie, was a stunning ring.

'Oh, my God! Oh, my God!' I burbled. 'What *is* this?'

I slid the ring off the scrunchie as Jock came back from the kitchen, grinning from ear to ear. He had clearly meant to give me a shock.

'Is this what I think it is?' I asked him, tears in my eyes.

'Of course, it's an engagement ring. I hope you like it – I drew it and then had it made in London for you.'

'Oh, Jock – it's beautiful!' I breathed, my eyes filling with tears.

'So – will you marry me?'

'*Yes!*' I shouted, flinging myself into his arms. 'Yes, yes, yes, yes!'

Chapter 20

A New Chapter

'I now pronounce you husband and wife,' the registrar said, smiling, with impeccable professionalism, indicating to Jock with an elegant sweep of the hand that he could now kiss me. We looked at one another, tears in our eyes, as he gathered me into his strong arms and planted a soft, passionate kiss on my lips.

'Yeurgh!' Steven exclaimed, and we all laughed. I say *all* – including the registrar, there were only seven of us in the room.

When Jock had asked me a few weeks earlier how I wanted our wedding to be, I had stared at him blankly. Until that moment, I hadn't even thought about the wedding. All I wanted was to be married to Jock – the idea of a big wedding filled me with dread.

'I want it to be small,' I said firmly, 'just us as a family. We don't have much money anyway and I don't like being the centre of attention, Jock.'

There was something else – I couldn't bear the thought of trying to get my whole family together and the stress and tension this would create. The idea was too hideous for words and I knew that whatever we chose, we were bound to upset somebody.

'This is for us, nobody else,' Jock insisted. 'So let's do things the way we want to do them. I've been through the big-white-wedding thing before and look how that worked out for me! I just want to be by your side, Tina.'

So, on 14 February 1996, Saint Valentine's Day, we married at Dundee Register Office – just us, the boys and our good friends, George and Jean. Jock was more handsome than ever in his suit and the boys looked great in their kilts; I wore a very simple but elegant Jackie Onassis-style black dress. We'd told our friends and family to meet us in Dad's bar at 3 p.m., under the pretext of a celebration for winning a big award for the pub.

No one suspected a thing until the moment we descended the stairs together, Jock looking dapper and me in my smart little dress. I think our grins and the way I held up my left hand gave it away. The penny dropped and a great roar erupted from the crowd of friends and colleagues.

Dad was serving pints at the moment of our arrival and, at first, he looked confused – then, when he caught my eye and saw I was beaming from ear to ear, his eyes welled up and he put up his hands to cover his mouth.

'Oh, no! Oh, no! You haven't, have you?' He started to weep then as he came out to congratulate us.

'Aye, Dad,' I said. 'We just got married.'

Dad could hardly speak – he was so overwhelmed. Then, after

he'd finished hugging us both, he disappeared into the cellar and came back with champagne for everyone. He and I drank Pepsi Max instead, since neither of us was drinking at this point. Gradually, as my sisters and Jock's family all filtered into the bar that afternoon, we broke the news over and over. Everyone was thrilled. I called my mum in England and, though she was upset she wasn't there, she was very happy for us. Of course, it would have been lovely to have our families with us for the wedding itself but, in the end, altogether, it was a beautiful day and just right for us: stress-free, simple and intimate.

Life as a family now moved on. Over the last few months, Steven and I had grown very close and I knew he missed his mum a lot. He had found her abandonment extremely difficult to handle and so I decided to try to help – I joined the panel that sat on the children's court. We were given lots of support, training and information to allow us to make the best decision for the children who came before us. And now I gained a greater insight into children's welfare and a better understanding to allow me to help Steven.

It also opened my eyes to the different ways children are affected by their backgrounds. We came across so many kids from divorced or fractured relationships and I saw how this impacted on children in different ways – I saw kids who had eating problems, drug problems, drink issues; violent children, disruptive children, all united by one thing: they had no outlet for their pain and confusion. I saw the many ways children tried to deal with catastrophic breakdowns in their young lives. There were even children who begged to be sent away from their families because of the destructive patterns and behaviours they were witnessing on a daily basis. It was so sad – but, at the same time, truly enlightening. For the first time, I got a window into my own behaviour as a child. I saw the mechanisms I had employed to try to cope and, now, I could look back with a degree of objectivity and see that my past behaviour was not in any way abnormal. It was greatly comforting.

At the same time, Steven was offered counselling through his school, which gave him the support he needed. We all worked together to help him adjust to the new situation and to process what had happened. I can't say it didn't affect him – of course it did – but I was so proud of the way he dealt with his feelings and privileged to be in a position to nurture, help and love him.

Just a few months later, I fell pregnant again. Though I was slightly nervous because of my previous miscarriage, we were both thrilled and I embraced the changes pregnancy brought and loved my new womanly shape. I kept myself fit and healthy and enjoyed the special feeling of knowing I was carrying a child inside me. By now, I was into homeopathy and various alternative medicines and had a very romantic view of childbirth. I suppose, without my mother to tell me differently, I envisaged it being a magical, transcendental experience.

On 19 January 1997, I was taken into hospital two weeks over my due date, to be induced, and I took with me a birth plan that included organic lavender oil, Bach flower remedies and a water birth. So convinced was I of the pureness of the birth, I told the midwives emphatically that I would not need any pain relief!

In the labour suite, Jock held my hand, massaged my back and whispered encouraging words. But we hadn't been in there long when I saw one of the nurses slip a bit of paper underneath the clear little cot, which had been brought in for the baby when it arrived.

'Jock, that piece of paper is about me!' I said, eyeing the note suspiciously once she had left the room. The way she had done it, covertly like that, I knew I was not meant to see what was in it.

'Don't be silly, Tina,' Jock said. 'You're being paranoid.'

I had to know – so I went over to the cot and fished out the little piece of paper. On it, she had written that I had a huge risk of developing postnatal depression.

It was a shock and, instantly, I remembered Pam and her baby, how she had let her cry and cry; the terrible thoughts she had of killing her. I was mortified that they thought this would happen to me but, worse than that, I was offended they hadn't thought to discuss this with me in advance of the birth. It felt like I was being treated like a child again, not trusted to rationalise and order my thoughts. Yes, it's true I was probably more at risk than most people but it would have been better for them to talk to me about it instead of passing clandestine notes to one another!

Still, I tried to put it out of my head and concentrate on the birth. I felt secure at this stage that the birth would be natural and beautiful. At one point, we heard a blood-curdling scream from the labour suite. I asked the nurse what was going on next door and she looked at me in surprise.

'That's a lady giving birth,' she said slowly, as if to a very dumb child. I shrugged – perhaps the woman had a low pain threshold and was overreacting?

A few hours later, the contractions started and I put myself in the bath with my lavender oils, thinking this would do the trick. But as each minute passed, the pains came on, stronger and harder. By the second hour of this, I was on my knees, doubled over in agony.

'Oh, Jesus!' I gasped, reaching out towards the nurse. 'Please give me some bloody pain relief – I can't handle this!'

'Darling, you're not even dilated yet. This is still the early stages of labour,' the midwife replied nonchalantly. *How could she be so damn cruel*, I thought. *I'm dying here!*

'Oh, Christ!' I screamed as another contraction drove hard against my stomach. 'There's no flipping way I'm having a damn water birth!' I exploded. 'And you can throw this crap away, too!' Picking up the Bach flower remedies, I flung them in the bin. I was furious – why didn't anyone tell me it was going to be this hard?

Jock couldn't help it – a wry smile passed over his face. After all the times I'd insisted I was going to have a natural birth, I was now begging the midwives for an epidural. After what felt like hours, I was finally given one, but it only worked on my left side so I was still in agony down the right side of my body. Oh, God, the pain was unbearable! I screamed, I fainted and I cried in pure agony. For 48 hours, I was in and out of consciousness, I was sick and my blood pressure kept dropping. Eventually, after a traumatic birth, my little boy arrived, born back to back, which is said to be the most painful way to deliver. He was nearly 10 lb, so no wonder I screamed! We called him John.

I knew from the word go that I was completely unprepared for motherhood emotionally. I had no idea I would be so traumatised by the birth but the love I felt for my son was immediate, overwhelming and like nothing I had ever experienced before. The intensity of the responsibility for this tiny, helpless creature was all on my shoulders. It was a shock and I begged my mum to come up and help me. Since Jock had to go back to work soon after the birth, I knew I needed the help.

The district nurses were on the watch for signs of PND – postnatal depression – and visited every day, to make sure I was coping okay. Sometimes, it was hard to know myself. I was recovering from the birth, sleep-deprived and utterly exhausted from worry, much of the time. It was amazing that so many women had gone through this terrifying, exhilarating experience before – how did they all cope?

'Don't worry,' my mum reassured me one night when I was fretting over John latching onto the breast. 'You're doing great. You're doing everything right, so don't worry about a thing.'

It was such a relief to have Mum there and, for the first time since I was a very little girl, I was reminded what a brilliant mother she had been to me. After all, she had raised four girls and knew exactly what to do and how to support me. In the wee hours of the morning, when I was practically a zombie from lack of sleep and John woke up screaming, she would often come in and take him from me, rocking him to sleep in the living room so I could get some rest. The way she nurtured my child reminded me of all her wonderful qualities before it had all gone so horribly wrong.

I wanted to be a really good mum myself – I was determined not to fail at this. If I'm being honest with myself, I'd say I probably did teeter on the edge of insanity for a while. I was terribly protective of John – if someone walked past us in the street with a cigarette, I was frightened he would choke on the smoke. I couldn't let anyone else feed or hold him except my mum or Jock, and I was obsessed with keeping him away from bacteria and germs.

'You've got to relax a bit more,' Jock urged one evening, as I got up to wash the changing table for the hundredth time.

'What are you talking about?' I snapped back. 'I'm fine!'

'You've cleaned that table fourteen times in the past two hours,' he observed drily. 'I don't call that normal, do you?'

'Mind your own beeswax!' I retorted. 'I just didn't get it clean the first time, that's all.'

'Well, I'm just saying, Tina, for your own sake, to take it easy once in a while. You know I wouldn't say anything to upset you – it's for your own good.'

That night, I replayed the conversation over in my head. *Are you meant to be relaxed in this situation*, I wondered. *How can any new mum relax when her baby is so small and dependent?* Yes, I knew I was fixated but I didn't judge myself to be ill. It was irritating that I had to keep proving myself to everyone in this way. Why couldn't they just accept I was fine? My history made everyone so jumpy around me. One thing I knew for certain, I wasn't going to have any more children in a hurry! So I went on the Pill.

After a couple of months, I was back in work. Fortunately, Steven and Danny were now both in school and I was able to take John into the bar with me and feed him in the office at the back. The bar was doing really well, so Dad decided to develop the upper part of the building, an old church, into a nightclub. He borrowed half a million pounds to get it up and running; he hired a top architect, sound engineers and went for the best of everything. The nightclub launch was wonderful and very exciting, as it was so much bigger than anything we had done before.

We used a promoter to get Snow Patrol, Biffy Clyro, Radio 1 live broadcasts, Judge Jules, Paul Oakenfold, Fergie and various other top DJs to always be on every other week.

Over the next year, I was very busy doing all I could to get the business going strong. But a year after having John, I fell pregnant again – once again the Pill had failed! It was such a shock, I didn't believe the doctor so, in June 1998, he sent me for a scan that revealed I was already five months pregnant. I really couldn't face going through another hellish birth, so I begged the midwives for a caesarean section. They refused – given the fact I was a strong candidate for PND, I was surprised at this reaction; so when I was overdue once again, I refused to go into hospital for the induction. But I couldn't put it off for ever – this baby *had* to come out! The night I went into hospital, I cried my eyes out, terrified of the pain to come.

As it was, when I went in, on 15 October 1998, it was all relatively easy and pain-free. They induced me, gave me an epidural and my beautiful baby girl, Holli, was born, pain-free, two hours later. I was so happy and excited, I asked to go straight home as I felt great, but they insisted I stay in overnight to make sure everything was okay. Jock brought the boys up at night and they loved Holli instantly.

When they all left, I made the most of the time alone to hold her, smell her skin and just look at her, taking in her beauty. She was my little baby girl and I was so happy! I knew what to do now so I wasn't daunted by the early demands of motherhood. We went home the next day and it was perfect.

I took a month off and then went back to work, taking my two little ones with me. Often I would have meetings and surreptitiously feed Holli under my top without anyone noticing. As the kids all grew, I would take them with me to the sound checks of the bands and DJs.

One day, after an unexpected visit from a health-and-safety officer, I decided to train for my NEBOSH certificate – the occupational-health-and-safety certificate. It was a 10-month course that actually benefited the business enormously and I was even approached to become a member of the Tayside Licensed Trade Association. The meetings were great – all the publicans were larger-than-life characters and so much fun! As I carved out a niche for myself, helping publicans with their health-and-safety policies, I loved every minute of it. Finally, I felt I had established myself as a success in this field. I had proved my worth and I belonged.

By now, Jock was working offshore as a technician so he was away a lot of the time. It wasn't always easy to manage the kids on my own while he was away and I was shattered most nights but, at the weekends, we were a family again and Dad was always there whenever I needed him. He was a huge part of my life now and the kids loved him, as did Jock. We even went away on holidays with Dad and his partner to Vegas, Lapland and Rome.

I had grown closer to Mum, too – over the years, she had made an effort to come and see the kids and me a lot. I loved her with all my heart but, still, the bond that had broken during my illness was never quite rebuilt. And it was during one of her visits that the barriers between us were finally torn down, once and for all.

Chapter 21

A Dark Family Secret

It was around 9 p.m., after the eldest kids had gone to bed, when Mum and I sat down in the living room for a well-deserved cup of tea.

'Thanks, Mum,' I said, blowing steam off the top of my mug. 'It makes such a difference when there are two adults around these days!'

The kids were different ages now but they all needed their fair share of attention, cuddles and bedtime stories. Mum's frequent visits during the weeks when Jock worked offshore were a godsend.

'Oh, you don't have to thank me, Tina,' Mum tutted. 'You know that I love it. And your kids are all adorable, all of them.'

'Aye, they can be adorable when they want to be. They can also be little horrors!' I recalled a two-hour stand-off the night before with John, who had refused to go to bed. He was a curious, alert child – even as a baby, he always had his eyes wide open, taking in everything around him. Now five, he was into everything and, at three years old, Holli was also asserting her independence. She was the youngest, the baby, but she wanted to prove she could do what the big boys did. I really had my hands full!

'No, don't say that,' Mum said, smiling indulgently, just a hint of sadness in her eyes.

'Aye, Mum – I'm only joking, you know that!'

Mum sat then and looked out into the distance, as if staring deep into the past. A heavy silence fell between us as she chewed on her lip – I could tell there was something on her mind.

'Tina, do you remember when you were younger, I told you I had a secret but I couldn't tell you it until you were much older?' she started.

Her words stirred vague memories from the past, of Mum laughing as I tried to wheedle her secret out of her.

'Yeah, I remember that,' I said. 'What was it, Mum?'

'Tina, I had a son,' she said simply, her eyes shining with an intensity I'd never seen before. 'When I was very young and before I met your father, I had a little boy. And I had to put him up for adoption, even though I didn't want to. I've spent my whole life thinking about him, Tina, praying he's okay, wanting to go back and change the past. But I couldn't.

'Tina, I'm so sorry I've not told you until now but it's been the great tragedy of my life and I have been deeply, deeply ashamed. I'm so sorry.'

At that moment, my mother broke down in tears and I

dashed over to the sofa to comfort her. I could hardly believe it. I had a brother? I was shocked and, at the same time, very distressed to see my mum so upset.

'Don't cry, Mum,' I whispered into her neck as I rubbed her back and held her. 'You don't have to apologise to me – just tell me what happened. I'd really like to know.'

Mum pulled her cardigan around her tightly and lifted up her head. Until now, I'd heard snippets about her early life, but not that much. She didn't like to talk about her childhood. I knew her parents had met and fallen in love while serving in the Army during the war. Mark was a bomb-disposal expert with the Royal Engineers and Rita was in the WAAF. Mum was the second eldest after William, with three younger brothers – Scott, Damon and Tony.

'It all went wrong after my father died,' Mum began. 'I was just fifteen and he passed away in his sleep, of a coronary thrombosis. We were living abroad at the time but had to move back to Glasgow. We were plunged into poverty. Me and your gran got jobs in a spinning factory to make ends meet and took it in turns looking after the young ones. But Gran didn't cope well – she turned to drink and she relied heavily on me to do all the childcare and housework. If I didn't do things the way she wanted, she shouted and hit me. The boys ran wild – I hated it. I felt more like a servant in the house, doing everything for Gran, including all the washing, cleaning and cooking, while she was drinking and partying. It was real Cinderella stuff.

'Anyway, I started going out at night, just to get away from it all. It wasn't long before I met Ged, a drummer in a local band, who was studying to be an engineer. We went out on a few dates and he was always trying it on, but I refused. Then, one night, we went out to a party and I had a little bit too much to drink. When I woke up the next morning, we were both in bed, naked. I was horrified and very upset – I refused to see Ged after that.

'At home, things were getting worse and it all got too much for me. I took an overdose. They found me in time and I had my stomach pumped at the local hospital. It was then the nurses came to me and said: "Do you know you're pregnant?" I was in shock – I had been a virgin until that one night with Ged. I was deeply ashamed and, also, terrified – I needed support, I needed my mum. But when I told her, she stood bolt upright and slapped me across the face.

'She shouted: "You whore!" before storming out the ward. I was mortified and devastated. I curled up into a ball and wondered what was I going to do; my life was a mess. We had nothing and now this! Ged came up to see me that evening and I told him the news. He was shocked but said the right thing to do would be to get married. I thought this was the answer.'

I listened, transfixed by Mum's words. It seemed so strange to hear about her difficulties and burdens as a teenager. And I empathised immediately. After all, I too had felt responsible for my younger siblings as a teenager. And as a distraught young girl, I had also tried to take my own life. I could see the similarities between us now so clearly. I wanted to reach out and take that young girl's hand – I wanted to reach back through time and reassure her, tell her everything was going to be okay. Show her all the wonderful things she had to look forward to. How many times had I curled up in a hospital bed, feeling bleak and unloved? Just like my mum! If only we could have seen into our futures.

Mum took a sip of her tea and smiled weakly at me – I could tell the worst was yet to come.

'I wanted to believe I could marry Ged and everything would be okay,' she said sadly. 'But then a nurse told me that my mother had arranged for me to be moved to thee Salvation Army Home for Unmarried Mothers. It was all decided for me and I didn't have any say because I was still sixteen and classed as a child. I was taken to the Great Western Road Salvation Army home for unmarried mothers the next day. They discussed all the possibilities with me and it was decided the best thing for the baby was adoption. I did not want to give up the baby, but felt I had nothing to offer the child at home. There was no way I'd be able to cope with a baby with no support. It killed me.

'Ged was fine with the adoption – he didn't want the baby anyway. Nobody knew about the pregnancy apart from Ged, my mother and brothers. This was our dark family secret, the shameful secret that no one was allowed to know about. I stayed at the Salvation Army home for seven months, until I gave birth to Robert on 8 December 1967. He was a beautiful baby and, from the moment I set eyes on him, I fell in love – I just fell for him completely.

'But I knew, from the second he arrived, the clock was ticking. I knew he was going to be taken from me and I couldn't stand that thought. I tried not to sleep, for I wanted as much time with him as I could. The nurses tried to reassure me about the adoption, saying it would be "much better for the baby", but I was torn apart. Even though it was frowned upon, I kept

Robert in the bed beside me and loved him every minute he was with me. I knew every inch of his little body – his hair, his eyes, his tiny toes and nails. I loved him with my whole body and soul – he was my blood and my bones.'

The tears coursed down Mum's cheeks now and I wiped away my own – I knew exactly how she felt. As a mother myself, I sensed the visceral stab in the pit of my stomach at the thought of someone taking my children away. This was horrifying.

Mum's voice was barely a whisper now as she looked beyond the world around her, looked far back into the past. 'I spent every second I could with Robert,' she continued. 'Each night praying that the nurses wouldn't find a family for him so he could stay with me for ever. I was desperate to bring him home but Gran dismissed the suggestion, saying we would be thrown out onto the streets if I tried to do that. "We couldn't afford another mouth to feed," those were her words. Nevertheless, Robert and I were inseparable for six weeks, until the nurse came and told me the news I was dreading: they had found "a wonderful family for Robert". I was in shock. I could not bear to be parted from my precious little boy, the one thing in my life I loved more than anything else. I prayed to my dad above to protect him, to keep us together by some sort of miracle. But it was not to be.

'Our last night together was heartbreaking. I lay beside him, watching him sleep, seeing his tiny chest moving up and down with each breath. I began to imagine him growing up into a man and having a lovely wife and his own children. I hoped and prayed he would grow up to be strong and healthy. The night melted away far too quickly – I hadn't slept a wink. In the morning, I bathed him and put him in his little Babygro, fed him and sang his favourite nursery rhymes to him as we waited. I kissed him and breathed him in. I was trying to absorb him, to imprint him into my mind so strongly that I would never forget his scent and skin. I held him tightly with his tiny little head cradled under my chin; his warmth was my strength.

'At two o'clock, a nurse came in with a bundle of paperwork. For a brief second, I saw sympathy in her eyes. She came over to me and put her arms out to take Robert. I stood up and walked over to the crib and put him in, covering him with his little white shawl, tucking in his little blue rabbit I had knitted for him. I bent over and kissed him one last time. The last kiss for the rest of my life to my son – then I ran out into the gardens. I lay on a bench, crying until I was sick. My whole body ached in pain with loss and grief. It was a pain I had never experienced before and one from which I've never recovered.

'That was the worst day in my whole life, Tina – the worst. When I returned to your gran's house, I couldn't bear to be around her a moment longer; I was filled with rage. I moved away and, eventually, at nineteen years old, I met your father. We were together for a few months when I told Michael about Robert, and I asked if he would help me get him back but he said, no, as it wouldn't be right for the child. In fact, it wouldn't have been possible anyway.

'Your father was also from a poor, working-class family but we fell in love and, for the first time in years, I had hopes for a bright future. More than anything else, I wanted a family. I wanted a settled, secure and happy life, to mend my broken heart.'

Suddenly, something clicked in my head. I could see now

why Mum had gone off the rails when she found out about my dad's infidelity. She had put all her hopes into this perfect family life they had created – she had buried all that hurt and pain by building a better life. For the first time, I understood fully now why she had been so destroyed by my dad's behaviour.

'So is that why you took it so badly?' I asked tentatively. 'You know, when Dad went off . . .'

'Yes, I suppose it was.' Mum nodded solemnly. 'I had never forgotten about Robert. Every day, I thought of him, of the age he would be now, and hoped he had a good life. But I tried to create a new life for myself, a perfect family life, and I thought I had succeeded. When it all came crashing down that dream was shattered, too, and the hurt went even deeper than before. The sense of betrayal was terrible and I couldn't forgive him for that.'

'How do you feel now, Mum? I mean, about what you did to Dad?' I had to know.

'Of course I regret it!' she said. 'I bitterly regret it. Your father forgave me years ago and, in some ways, we are learning to put the past behind us now and create a friendship. I mean, I did love him, after all, and he is your father. I just thought it was time for you to know what lay behind all of that. You deserve to know the truth – after all, Robert is your half-brother and, who knows, he may come looking for his birth family one day.'

We sat in silence then; Mum all talked out, me trying to absorb the enormous news she had just revealed. It was so sad that she had kept this secret for so long – that she had been made to feel ashamed, that she had been forced to give up her child. My heart went out to her. Now I could see the links between us, the way both of us had fought our own instability and uncertainties about the future. All that time I had imagined myself battling on my own to overcome my mental ill health, I realised now that Mum, too, had fought her own battles. And like me, she'd snapped.

At the same time, I was excited to learn I had an older brother and my mind swarmed with questions: Would he look like me? Where was he now? Would he want to know all of us?

'I've tried to find him, Tina,' Mum said after a while, pushing the hair back from her face. 'All the agencies, the organisations – you know, I've been to all of them but I don't seem to be able to get anywhere. It's up to him – if he wants to find us, he will. In the meantime, I miss him. You know? After all these years, Tina, I actually miss him.'

I took my mother in my arms then and held her as she sobbed like a child. For the first time in our lives, we had reached a level of understanding and compassion that had never really been there before. She had suffered so much and, now, I could see and feel the scars of her past – I loved my mother more than words could ever say.

Chapter 22

Losing Dad

Over the next few years, our lives settled into a happy rhythm. I was fulfilled both personally and professionally and I felt mentally strong. Occasionally, I still thought about flying but, for now, I had to concentrate on raising the children and, while they were young, I didn't feel it was right to put myself in a position of unnecessary risk. I reassured myself that, one day, I would get back up in a plane.

Jock and I were busy with the kids and work but we stayed close to all the members of the family. We all tried to help Mum find Robert but, sadly, got nowhere. However, she was very contented in her life and was even made mayor in her town! It was such an achievement and we were all very proud. I couldn't help but feel a little amazed at the turnaround – after all, she had been in prison years before. Now, that was firmly in the past. We all went down for her inauguration ceremony and it was excellent. Reg, her husband, looked wonderful in his new suit and she looked radiant with pride as they were both given their chains of office.

The onset of Dad's health problems coincided with our business difficulties. He had stopped drinking and smoking years before after a couple of mini-strokes but, when the business started to fail, he fell back into bad habits. A smoking ban in bars introduced in 2006 hit us hard. Then, two other bars owned by big pub companies opened within a few hundred yards of us, with cut-price drinks and food. The supermarkets were competing on our turf, too, offering ridiculous prices for alcohol. It meant everyone was staying at home to drink and smoke instead of coming to the pub.

Over the next year, our turnover went down and the interest payments on our loans went up. The global financial meltdown began to impact on every small business and we were in trouble. Before then, I could pay everyone on time and in full. Now, Dad said I could only pay bits and pieces to keep the wolves from the door.

Eventually, the crash came late in 2006, and we lost everything. We had to sell the business for next to nothing. Dad's collection of top-of-the-range BMWs was repossessed and he was left humiliated and broke. It was awful and very degrading.

A year later, Dad decided he needed an income again, so he invested every penny into a rundown bar in Dundee that had been closed for a very long time. We tried to talk him out of it as it was going to be a tough call. But running a bar was all he knew and loved, and he was convinced he could make it a success. The day he signed the papers, he was a wreck, sweating profusely and shaking like a leaf. I took him aside, to ask him if he knew what he was doing, and he just said: 'Yes, Tina, I have no choice.'

It was always going to be a disaster. We tried our hardest to make it work, putting in long hours and every ounce of energy we had but, by now, Dad was showing strange signs. He was walking oddly, shuffling along, barely picking up his feet. When he went to the doctor, he was told that he needed a knee replacement but, at fifty-eight, he was too young. A year on, he was slurring his words. The doctors said this was down to mini-strokes but reassured him that he was essentially fine, putting him on a course of statins, fish oils, and glucosamine for his knees.

But I could see he was getting worse and worse. Now, his legs were so stiff, he had to pull them one at a time into the car in the mornings. His knees were solid and could hardly move; his face was also becoming expressionless. Often, he would cry out in pain but would try to hide it from me, although I could see what was going on.

One day, I watched him try to tie his tie, but it was such a struggle for him, I decided to arrange an appointment with our family doctor. She gave him a small test, where she asked him to write his name, draw some pictures and answer some basic questions, before he had to get up and tie his shoelaces. He stood up and staggered over, but he could not tie his laces since his fingers would not work properly. The doctor instantly knew what was wrong with him.

'Michael,' she said. 'I'm going to refer you to the Parkinson's clinic for an assessment.'

No one had suffered from Parkinson's in our family, so I knew very little about the condition, apart from that the actor and activist Michael J. Fox had it, as did the great boxer, Muhammad Ali, and they were still alive after years, so I was not overly worried. I drove Dad home, then went back to our house and started researching on the Internet. The message seemed to be the same from every source – Parkinson's was a long-term degenerative illness but you don't die from it, which made me feel much happier as it meant it was not going to kill him and he would be around for a very long time, possibly disabled but at least alive and functioning. We knew that he was struggling at work so my sisters Katie and Sophie took over running the bar.

But Dad was stubborn – he refused to give up work until, one day, he could no longer walk up the stairs to the bar. We told him he needed to be at home to rest and he was devastated – it was all he had done for 22 years. He loved his job and all the people he saw every day, but he could no longer walk and the staff and customers were struggling to understand him when he spoke.

The clinic diagnosed vascular Parkinson's, which was probably brought on by his arrhythmia and mini-strokes, the latter brought on by minuscule clots of blood created by the irregular heart rhythm hitting his brain. The drugs they gave him made practically no difference at all. He was also given intensive physiotherapy and hydrotherapy.

Meanwhile, the bar was losing money fast. The recession had hit everyone and our community could no longer afford a regular night at the pub, so, reluctantly, we closed the doors in 2010. I was lucky as I was working as a phlebotomist by then, my sister Katy had started a small cleaning company and Sophie had gone back to working in pubs, so we all had other sources of income; but it broke Dad's heart to know his bar life was over.

Just a year later, he was fully in the grip of the disease. It was frightening how quickly it progressed – he could hardly walk at all now and his legs were so rigid and almost bow-shaped, he needed a Zimmer frame to move a few feet. His bones now made a creaking noise, which was horrible. The pain would often bring tears that rolled softly down his face, without him making a sound. But he never complained.

Dad's voice was also disappearing. All the muscles in the voice box and larynx were affected, depriving him of the ability to speak. He was in Victoria Hospital for a few months and, there, they confided his illness was one of the fastest they had ever seen in the unit. It got so bad, his swallow reflex was affected and he started choking on his medication and food. This led to several bouts of pneumonia – it was very distressing for him and us.

We went to see him every night and I would sit and chat to him about my day and what the kids were up to. My other sisters would try to get up during the day and he loved seeing everyone. He had a portable DVD player and spent every day sitting, watching films – it was really all he could do now. Dad was now in adult nappies and, on what the doctors described as, a Stage C diet to stop him choking. This consisted of mushy food – thickened fluids – so all his tea or water looked like wallpaper paste, yoghurt and custard. He could not eat anything else as it would stick in his throat or go straight into his windpipe. It took him about an hour to eat a tiny plate of mashed food, so we would just all sit together and eat and chat.

Dad was now a true invalid. It killed me to see him this way – after all, he used to be the life and soul of the bar, with a joke and a smile for everyone. Now, he barely saw anyone and, too ill to live at home, he was put into a room in a rehabilitation unit. I couldn't help reflecting on the circles in our lives – 20 years previously, it had been me in the rehab unit. Now, it was Dad. He needed a hoist now as his body had become so rigid he couldn't straighten his legs at all any more. His arms would get stuck in a V-shape and his fingers refused to close. His sharp mind and mischievous wit were trapped in a useless body.

When he was sixty-one, he was admitted to hospital from the unit with a respiratory infection, unable to breathe. When I came to see him, a consultant took me aside for a quiet word.

I was nervous as I followed him into the small side room.

'Mrs McGuff, you have to understand your father is a very sick man now,' he started. 'I think you and your family should be prepared for the fact that it is unlikely he will last another year.'

'*What?* How do you know that?' I demanded. I didn't want to believe him.

'I have been doing this job for thirty-five years, Mrs McGuff. We know from previous cases and Parkinson's, that's the pattern. I'm sorry. I know it's the last thing you want to hear, but you need to get power of attorney as well. Please go and see your lawyer.'

'*No!*' I replied tartly. 'My father is of sound mind and can make his own decisions and, until the day he can't, I'm not going to do anything.'

The consultant fixed me with a knowing look then, and said: 'Look, it's not about the illness – my wife has power of attorney over me in case I drop dead. It's just to ensure you can deal with the legal matters without any issues.'

'Okay, well, thank you, Doctor. I'll talk to my sisters about it,' I said. But I couldn't accept his words. I was convinced my dad would soldier on for a lot longer.

But he continued to slide downhill – after a few months, he was choking on everything and he could not speak at all. He communicated through pointing to letters on a piece of paper. During this time, he lost a lot of weight, since he was barely eating, and was also given a long-term catheter so they could measure every liquid input and output. We went to see him every day – I was determined to be there for him, to show him my love. From my own experience, I knew just how lonely and bleak it was, living in a hospital ward. It was his love that had saved me all those years before – I would be there for him, too. I couldn't let him down.

At night, I lay awake, unable to sleep for worry. We all loved him so much – he was the glue that held our family together and my best friend. I thought about all our amazing times together as a family and how the grandchildren adored his silliness and jokes. I missed him moaning at me for not going fast enough around the cash-and-carry in the mornings, and the Sunday lunches at the house. It was all slipping away and I was not ready for that.

A few months later, the doctor called us all in for a conference.

'Your father is dying,' she told us with sorrow in her eyes. 'He doesn't have long now: once the swallow reflex goes, as his has, he can choke on his own saliva. This is a potentially life-threatening issue. He could choke to death or develop pneumonia again and not pull through.'

It was our worst fears confirmed. She asked us whether we wanted to keep admitting Dad to Ninewells Hospital when he was ill and we all looked at each other and agreed instantly that we would do whatever Dad wanted. He still had a fully working mind and, if he chose to stop treatment, we would accept and abide by his decision. We asked if Dad knew all of this and she said, yes, if he had a heart attack now, he'd chosen not to be resuscitated. We had no choice – we had to respect Dad's wishes.

My sisters and I were all devastated – I could see from their anguished expressions, we felt the same way. I suddenly felt very detached from the situation, light-headed almost.

'Your father knows he is dying,' the doctor added. 'We have been mentally preparing him for a month or so.'

It was like being smashed in the face with a sledgehammer. I felt my chest tighten and thought I was going to faint. Tears streamed down all our faces, there in the room. This was the news I had dreaded and I just blocked it out. Even though I was hearing the words, I pretended it wasn't happening. The doctor asked us to all have a chat and speak to Dad, then get back to her with our wishes. *This can't be real*, I thought, recalling my online research. *You don't die from Parkinson's disease. Maybe he'll recover?*

She left us and we talked – we were united; we would go

along with whatever Dad wanted. We went to see him and I asked him if he was okay. He looked at me with a knowing expression and nodded slowly; he knew what this was about.

'Dad, we just wanted you to know that we have agreed to do whatever you want,' I said in a tremulous voice. 'If you wish to stop treatment, then we'll respect that.'

Dad nodded again. I knew for certain then he didn't have long: his head was now stuck in a forward position as his neck muscles were frozen. His whole body was rigid. He spent all day and night in bed, hoisted up only now and again to have a bath and get his nappies changed. I burst into tears and tried to hug him – he was crying, too. He tried to say something, so I got up and went for a sheet of paper.

He spelt out the words: 'You are crushing my neck!' which made us all laugh. Typical Dad! He had a silly sense of humour and that's what got us through a harrowing moment.

Now we knew how Dad wanted to die: he wanted to go home, to see the view of the River Tay from his window and feel surrounded by love and care. He didn't want his last moments to be in a sterile hospital ward. We had a wonderful care manager and the palliative care plan started taking shape. It was terrible, knowing we were making plans for his death. I prayed there would be some sort of problem and they could not get him home so he would be kept alive in the ward and we could still see him every day. I went to see him just before his sixty-second birthday, one night on my own, and was sitting next to him.

'Dad, can you not stay here a little longer?' I asked quietly.

He looked at me and whispered in a tiny voice, a voice that

took him so much effort to summon up: 'Tina, they can't keep me here for ever.'

And he was right. Selfishly, I wanted him to live longer but he was exhausted and wanted it all to end. On the eve of his return home, Celine made the massive 24-hour bus journey up from her home in Cornwall, heavily pregnant.

Dad was brought back to his house on 20 March 2011, a week after his 62nd birthday. His bedroom had been transformed into a medical suite, with a large hospital bed, mechanical hoist, oxygen cylinders, nappies and tons of equipment. We were all there when he arrived in a huge ambulance, lying flat for he was too ill to sit up. He looked awful – very grey and scared, and his breathing was terrible. We tried to smile at him but we could see from his eyes he was frightened he might not make it into the house. He was very carefully brought in on a stretcher.

We all went into his room, where the nurses stabilised him, then carefully and slowly, they hoisted him into his bed. We had decided to take it in turns, sleeping in his room on the floor, and had brought in some sofas and mattresses. Katie had even hooked up a massive flat-screen TV so he could watch whatever he wanted. It was cosy and comfortable.

The nurses were there 24 hours a day in two-hour shifts, ensuring he always had enough morphine to keep the pain at bay. We were emphatically told not to call 999 in an emergency. He was dying and had asked for no resuscitation, so they would not come for him. It was all so very real now, so final.

Dad was now able to see out of the window and he looked happy. We all sat with him around the clock and, for the first few days, we felt upbeat as he was still communicating. His friend John visited a lot and we all sat and joked around, making sure he was included in every conversation.

The nurses and carers were all brilliant – and our family doctor came, too, to check on him. It was a very special and precious time for all of us. We sat and held his hand as, every day, he grew weaker and weaker. No longer able to move, he pretty much stayed on his side. He slept a lot and someone always sat on the chair next to him and held his hand.

Celine stayed as long as she could, but she had to get back down to Cornwall as she was due any day. She said a private goodbye to Dad, knowing she would never see him again. We took her to the bus station and promised to call her every day with updates. We were all worried about her as it was such a long journey. She told me she cried all the way home.

One day, Dad opened his eyes and started making noises, trying to tell everyone to get out and that he was in a lot of pain. Katy, my sister, and Auntie Annette, who were both there, called the nurses – they calmed him down and increased his sedation. The nurses explained that in the final days, it was common to have strange reactions and pains.

The next day, Dad woke up and smiled, and started picking at his sheets. It frightened me as I had read on one of the websites that this was a sign that death was close. I cried silently and never said a word. Dad was sleeping more and more, and could not even do the thumbs-up now so, to communicate, we held his hand and he answered by squeezing our hands with his thumb. He was slipping away from us and there was nothing we could do apart from be there, so he could hear us, and give him some comfort in his final days.

I had a prescription to take to the chemist, which the nurses had left. The pharmacist behind the counter took it from me and, after he'd read it, I saw him look up at me with sadness. When it was ready, he called me over, took my hand and said: 'I'm sorry.' This stranger's sympathy moved me greatly, and I thanked him before leaving, extremely upset but touched by his small token of kindness.

By 27 March 2011, Dad was not even able to squeeze our hands any more. Now he was in a very, very deep sleep. He did not stir at all and his skin looked different. His nasal oxygen tube was now switched off – there was no point in it being there. We knew it would not be long.

The following night, I sat next to him, knowing I would never see him again. I couldn't face the final moment of death and had asked my sisters if they were okay with this. They said of course. I also told them that I would not be able to get involved with the funeral arrangements – I recognised my mental state was now very fragile. I was only just holding myself together.

Danny and Jock came along that night, as did John, Dad's lifelong friend. I held Dad's hand for hours. The nurses came in at about 11 p.m. and told me in the hall that they could tell from his breathing that he was in the final stage. I stayed there until 12.30 a.m. of 29 March and kissed my dad for the very last time. It tore me apart, knowing that I would never see my father again. I did not want to leave – I just kept touching his hand and looking at his skin and fingers and remembering all the times he had held my hand as a little girl – the times he held my hand in hospital when I was younger – and now I was holding his hand to say goodbye for ever.

Finally, I dragged myself away and we drove home in silence, my mind full of memories.

I woke at 4.45 a.m. the next morning and lay there for a while, thinking about Dad. At 5.30, my phone rang – it was Katie.

'Tina, he's gone,' she said simply. She couldn't say anything more and neither could I – we were both too upset. I called Celine to break the news and, strangely, she too had woken early – at 4.30 a.m. – and was sitting in her lounge, thinking of Dad.

After I put down the phone, I fell apart, crying for hours and hours. The pain in my body was unbelievable; my heart ached in my chest. Jock held me and then Danny came through and lay with me, hugging me for an hour. John and Holli also came through and we all cried together.

I felt numb and, all day, I stayed in bed, crying – I did not want to leave my room to see anyone. Jock let everyone else know, for I was unable to talk to anyone. I could not speak for days without bursting into tears. If ever there was a time my mental strength would be tested, it was now – this was the moment I was dreading.

I told my best friend Keren that I didn't think I could cope with going to the funeral – I just wasn't strong enough. Keren suggested we go to Glamis Castle during the funeral so I could say my goodbyes to Dad in my own way. Alongside my children and my wonderful friend, we walked through the grounds and reminisced together. It was a very special morning.

The funeral was held at Dundee crematorium, where we arranged to have some of Dad's favourite songs played: 'Love On The Rocks' by Neil Diamond and 'Lola's Theme' by The Shapeshifters. Dad's great friend Graham gave the eulogy (Jock recorded the audio for me so I could listen to it when I felt strong enough). The crematorium was packed with all Dad's friends, family and customers, and Graham recalled some hilarious stories – just what we all wanted for our dad.

Life went back to normal very slowly after that. I could not go to his house for months, and when I did, I could not look in his bedroom. Every time I spoke about him, I would cry. I found my father's death very difficult to deal with, but I just tried to get on with life as best I could and as I knew he would have wanted me to.

This was a very frightening time for my family – they told me later they feared I would have another breakdown. Dad and I had grown so close as adults – all the trauma and difficulties of my upbringing were a world away from the close, supportive relationship we had built in later years. Thankfully, my family needn't have worried: I was grieving, yes – obviously, I was distraught at the loss of my father – but thanks to everything I had been through, thanks to the doctors and nurses who had taught me so much – and with the love and support of my family and friends – I was absolutely fine. I was mentally strong.

A month after Dad died, Celine and Sophie both gave birth to little boys. It was sad that Dad never got to meet them but the new additions brought some much-needed joy and excitement to all our lives.

Three years on and I still miss my dad but I am ploughing on with my life, working hard and giving talks to psychology students about anorexia. It was important to me that I put my own experiences to good use. The kids have all grown into fine adults and teenagers, and make me proud every day. Mum is happier and busier than ever; Katie now lives in Dubai, working as a real-estate agent. Sophie, too, is doing well after a long and difficult battle with drug addiction. She is a single parent of two children and is now back at college. Celine is settled in Cornwall with her husband and two kids, and works for a hotel. All us girls have fought our own battles, marked as we were by an unsettled childhood, but we have come through our experiences stronger as individuals and stronger as a family.

Every day, I look at my life and I feel so lucky. There are moments when I feel grateful that I am here – living, loving and cherishing the special people in my life. It has been a long and difficult journey at times, but also magical and wonderful and, one thing I know for certain, I wouldn't have missed any of it for the world. Best of all, I know there's so much more good stuff to come!

Epilogue

Today, I look back at my life and my 'ill time' and I can't believe it was me – I lost so much and gained very little. My pseudo-friend anorexia cost me my friends, family, self-esteem, teenage years, education and nearly my life. Hence the reason I'm so blessed to have what I have now. I wrote it all down in the hope it will be helpful to others with any of the issues I have been through.

A huge lesson I have learned from my experiences is that beauty truly does come from within. You need to learn to respect and accept yourself for who you are in order to be truly happy. Confidence and contentedness will follow.

There is huge pressure in today's society and media to look a certain way – to have the so-called 'perfect' body. But no one could ever achieve this, for it is simply not possible. We need to create realistic role models our children can emulate and stop defining ourselves by our looks and bodies. Every day, there are women and men being torn down in the papers and magazines because they have 'cellulite' or 'man boobs'. Who cares? Let us live in peace! We are all unique and our bodies do not define the person we are inside.

I compare mental illness to an empty vessel that needs water drops to fill it. The advice and counselling I received were all little drops and they filled me with all I needed to become complete and whole again. In my experience, the best way of dealing with difficult situations is to talk. Talking is a massive healer – you may not realise it at the time but a counsellor or someone giving you advice and talking to you is giving you drops to add to your empty vessel. Every time you talk to someone, a tiny drop will go in, and, every time you hear advice, it's giving you a drop. They may be tiny drops and seem insignificant at the time but they all add up. Don't be scared to seek help or advice – nothing bad ever came from asking for help, only good. It may take time, but what do you have to lose?

Anorexia is treatable and does not have to be a death sentence. With the right therapy and support, it *is* possible to beat the illness. Every single case is different but there is usually a common thread. Often it is sparked by a situation that a person feels they can't control, whether at home, school or at work.

It is important to remember that it takes a long time to become 'ill' and it can also take a long time to become 'better'. Therefore, the sooner someone seeks help, the better. Psychological issues can take years to treat. I know there are new techniques used to treat anorexia but it appears the method that was used on me is still successful, so it's important for others to know this is what they may go through if they become very ill. I'm sure if I'd read my account in that book years ago, it may have stopped me from allowing the illness to take the grip on me that it did. At the very least, I'm convinced I would have asked for help more quickly.

Friends and family are key but only if they are a positive influence. One of my favourite quotes is: 'Those who mind, don't matter, and those who matter, don't mind.' It's very true. If your family or friends are part of the problem, then they are not part of the solution – get rid of negativity in your life! Positive influences are crucial in aiding recovery.

You only live once and so you need to appreciate yourself as a person and all you are worth. Everyone is worthy of love and support; the basic requirements of life need to be fulfilled in order for you to become more contented in the world. I learned this when I read Maslow's *Hierarchy of Needs*. To me, it makes sense and I include it here in the hope it may help someone else.

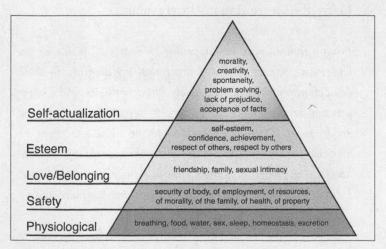

Self-actualization: morality, creativity, spontaneity, problem solving, lack of prejudice, acceptance of facts

Esteem: self-esteem, confidence, achievement, respect of others, respect by others

Love/Belonging: friendship, family, sexual intimacy

Safety: security of body, of employment, of resources, of morality, of the family, of health, of property

Physiological: breathing, food, water, sex, sleep, homeostasis, excretion

The fact is this: mental illness affects 1 in 4 people at some time in their lives. It is common and should be accepted and dealt with in the same way as physical illness, not hidden away. It is part of the human experience – for that reason, I think it should be called something else. Perhaps we should call it 'a slight blip', as my granny used to say. It is not 'another world' and, therefore, shouldn't be a taboo subject.

I hope that, in relaying my experiences, others, perhaps friends and family members, can become more aware of those potentially suffering. In short, let's all pay attention to each other. If someone gets the flu or a sniffle, they are straight to the doctor. It should be the same with mental illness – in fact, more so, as 'a slight blip' can have fatal consequences, unlike the common cold. Approximately 1.6 million people in the UK are affected by eating disorders. It is my great hope that in my lifetime this figure will drop significantly. This book is my way of helping to achieve that.

I leave the last word to my lovely mum:

I didn't realise what was happening to Tina until it was far too late – and, because of that, I nearly lost my daughter. In those days, anorexia was still a relatively unknown illness. All I knew was that my daughter had lost weight very quickly. A magazine article about Karen Carpenter made me think she might be anorexic but, knowing so little about the disease and how to handle it, I simply confronted Tina and she denied it, of course. I didn't understand what was going on in her head and had no way of getting through to her.

Before she was first admitted to hospital, I was on the phone to the doctor every week, but he said he couldn't do anything until she asked for help herself. Eventually, when she had a pain in her stomach and asked for the doctor, I was so relieved. He was there with the ambulance within half an hour, having organised a hospital bed. But she refused to go. I was devastated. We had to wait again. A week later, she collapsed in agony on the floor and called for help. This time, she went to hospital.

We got to the hospital and they took her in and explained that nobody could visit her until she had put on a certain amount of weight. She wasn't allowed to listen to the radio or to watch TV. She would be escorted to the toilet, to make sure she wasn't sick. There was a whole host of rules.

I was so grateful and relieved that she was in hospital, but it struck me as very cruel that she wasn't allowed to have family visits. It upset me to think she would assume we had abandoned her and didn't care. It was also hard to explain to her sisters why we couldn't visit her. Nevertheless, I was completely in the dark about this illness and I knew I had to follow the doctor's advice to give Tina the best chance of recovery.

She didn't know it at the time but I visited frequently, taking things up to the hospital in the hope of catching a glimpse of my daughter. But they wouldn't allow me in. The first time we were allowed an official family visit, we were told to keep things light and happy. It killed me having to say how great she looked and how well she was doing – it was clear she was a wreck; she was dying! Her father and I left the hospital completely heartbroken.

There were many setbacks during the years of Tina's illness and some truly terrifying moments – it took a long time but, finally, she beat her anorexia and we were all so proud of her. Today, I *am brimming with pride for the person she has become – she is a wonderful woman, a wonderful wife and mother. I am proud, too, that she has written this book to help others.*

In hindsight, I look back and blame myself. I put my children through more than they should have seen in their young lives, but I didn't appreciate at the time the impact of our changed circumstances on my daughters. We didn't even think about getting counselling for the girls or any help whatsoever. It wasn't suggested to us either. Back then, these things weren't an option but, if I'd given them counselling, I am certain Tina wouldn't have become anorexic.

I know I put too much on her shoulders. I should have realised, as her mother, she wasn't coping with her life and that she was very unhappy. I regret letting this happen to her and for being the cause of her trauma. I just hope that she will forgive me for taking that time out of her life because I will never forgive myself.

I say to all mothers, even though you love and care for your children, if there is ever any kind of trauma in their lives or any kind of change in your child, take them to counselling. Get some help before the problem escalates and takes a young life. Anorexia, like a great many mental illnesses, can kill. I wish I knew then what I know now and can only hope that, in sharing this terrible experience, Tina and I can offer at least one child the chance of a better life.

Support
and Advice

www.thenewmaudsleyapproach.co.uk – The New Maudsley Approach is a resource for professionals and carers of those with eating disorders.

www.b-eat.co.uk – Beat provides helplines, online support and a network of UK-wide self-help groups, to help adults and young people in the UK beat their eating disorders.

www.nbp-eating-disorders.co.uk – No Bodies Perfect (NBP) provides support, information and awareness of eating disorders in Scotland.

www.samaritans.org – The Samaritans is a confidential crisis organisation, offering support to those in need.

www.mind.org.uk – Mind offers information, support, advice and local groups to help anyone experiencing a mental-health problem.

www.childline.org.uk – ChildLine is a confidential, free counselling service on the phone and online for any child wanting to talk about issues affecting them.

www.seemescotland.org – See Me Scotland is a charity whose vision is to end mental-health stigma and discrimination, enabling people who experience mental-health problems to live fulfilled lives.

Acknowledgements

Thank you so much to all the nurses who looked after me and kept me alive against the odds. You will never know how thankful I am to you all.

Posthumous thanks to an amazing woman – Dr Barbara Ballinger, OBE, MRCP, MRCPsych (1941–2010) – I owe you a depth of gratitude and wish I could have told you this in person.

Thank you to my friend Keren and her family for always supporting my family – we love you, guys.

A massive thank you to Graham, who gave me hours of help and encouragement going forward. Without this, I may never have got to print.

Thank you also to Jane for reading for me. Your input was invaluable and appreciated.

Thank you to everyone I met along the way and helped

shape me to become who I am today. You have all left your mark on my memory and I will never forget you.

A huge thank you to Katy and Andrew for believing in me and my story. I'm forever grateful.

I would also like to thank and pay tribute here to my mum and sisters. I love you all from the bottom of my heart and I am sorry for everything I put you through.

Lots of love to my Auntie A and cousins . . . you know I love you all very much.

Big love to Uncle D and the rest of the clan . . . love you all, too.

A special thank you to my wonderful Italian family.

Dad – Rest in peace and I miss you every day.

Gary, for being there for me – love you.

I thank my children – Steven, Danny, John and Holli. You are all my favourites! I love you and you make me so proud to be your mum.

Thanks, too, to my nieces, nephew and TGJCH – love you all very much.

And thank you the most to my husband, Jock – you have always supported me and walked alongside me through tough times, never judging me or doubting me. Forever yours – FBS x